TOO SOON TO TELL

TOO SOON TO TELL

Calvin Trillin

FARRAR STRAUS GIROUX

NEW YORK

Library of Congress Cataloging-in-Publication Data
Trillin, Calvin.
Too soon to tell / Calvin Trillin.
p.   cm.
I. Title.
PS3570.R5T75   1995   814'.54—dc20   94-24629   CIP

Most of the columns in this book were originally
published through the King Features Syndicate, and
the others were first published in The New Yorker.

In memory of

ANDREW D. KOPKIND,

who was, in fact, the funniest of all

CONTENTS

Introduction, 3
Family Business, 9
A New Arrival, 12
Return of the Rubes, 15
Worms Turning, 18
Talk About Ugly!, 21
Special Dish, 24
Agents, Agents Everywhere, 27
Time and Tide, 30
Iowa on My Mind, 33
Believable History, 36
Sound Policy, 39
Stargazing, 42
Adventures in the Book Game, 45
The Alice Tax, 48
Check Him Out, 51
Women, Women, 54
Lip-Synching, 57
Truth Is Stranger, 60
A Traditional Family, 63
Gecko Redux, 66
Dog-Bark Duet, 69

Keeping Up with Geography, 72
Frog Theories, 75
Mass Exit, 78
Rock Threat Subsides, 81
Naming the German Baby, 84
The Past and the Future, 87
Go to Your Room, 90
International Chigger Alert, 93
Chinese Golf, 96
Please Stop, 99
Errands, 102
Polite Society, 105
Who Was First?, 108
I'm O.K., I'm Not O.K., 111
Planted Questions, 114
Counting My Blessings, 117
Too Old, 120
Speak Softly, 123
Orlando When It Sizzles, 126
A Visit from Jean-Michel, 129
Blues Blues, 132
Don't Mention It, 135
Bad Language, 138
Searching for the Elite, 141
Merger, 144
Women and Clubs, 147
Folktale, for Real, 150
The Right to Bear Chain Saws, 153
New Worries, 156
Broken English, 159

Taxing the Queen, 162

Networking for Fun and Profit, 165

Just Plain Bill, 168

Smoking Incorrectly, 171

Presidential Symbols, 174

Seat Belts for Dogs, 177

Capital Goobers, 180

Tabloid in the Tabloids, 183

Contemplating the Zoo, 186

Steven the Turtle, 189

Tough Enough, 192

Hurt Feelings, 195

In Defense of Sleeping, 198

Doubly Generous, 201

Alas, Poor Willy, 204

Little-Known Facts, 207

New Professor, 210

The Hot Stuff Cure, 213

Unmasked, 216

A Christmas Shopping Tale, 219

Pacific Insults, 222

Networkers Triumphant, 225

Exchanging Information, 228

Unplugged, 231

Out of Style, 234

Dangerous Machines, 237

Movie Reality, 240

Din! Din! Din!, 243

Beware of Pickpockets, 246

Eye of the Beholder, 249

Brutal Attack on Barney, 252
Nerds, Unvanished, 255
Hazardous Dining, 258
Embarrassment of Riches, 261
Questions about Prince Charles, 264
Jeff Again, 267
The Piping Plover, 270
So, Nu, Dr. Freud, 273
Hat Trick, 276
Sign Writing, 279
Video Talk, 282
What's the Good Word?, 285
Afterword, 289

TOO SOON TO TELL

I have found myself dealing with animals more than I'd expected to. That's what I'd say if some graduate student with a lot of time on his hands decided to go around asking newspaper columnists what they had found surprising about working their rather ramshackle side of the street.

"Do you mean you've written quite a bit about Chelsea Clinton's cat, Socks?" he would presumably ask.

I do not mean that. I am not without faults, but I have never written a word about Chelsea Clinton's cat, Socks. I was almost as restrained in my coverage of Barbara Bush's dog, Millie, even though Millie published a best seller. I can't even recall the name of Nancy Reagan's pet, although, as I remember, it was by Adolfo.

I did not set out to deal with any sort of animals, wild or domesticated or designer. I don't mean that I think of myself as having any greater than normal fear or loathing of animals. When I was a boy, I had a dog. When I kick at a cat, it's nearly always for good reason. It's true that many years ago I was attacked by a red-winged blackbird, but—to distinguish that episode from Jimmy Carter's encounter with a killer rabbit—I was never under the impression that I had been singled out. The attack took place not long after the release of Alfred Hitchcock's *The Birds*, and I concluded that the movie must have got around to the drive-ins: birds were seeing it and getting ideas. I bear no grudges.

Of course, there's nothing wrong with writing about animals now and again. In a column years ago, I acknowledged that I was having a terrible time keeping the raccoons out of the garbage until an old-timer in our town finally informed me that the secret of an effective raccoon defense was a combination lock ("They're cunning, but they've got no head for figures"). I've often mentioned that the tour of Lower Manhattan I provide for out-of-town visitors has featured as its principal attraction that savvy chicken on Mott Street capable of beating all comers at tic-tac-toe ("Yes, of course the Statue of Liberty is interesting, but wait till you see this . . ."). I have dealt with the question of whether placing bars of Ivory soap in the garden—perhaps bars that have been carved into flower-blossom shapes, so that they resemble a new strain of hybrid marigolds—is effective in keeping deer from eating the begonias, and if so, whether that has something to do with the fact that Ivory floats. I envisioned a deer backing off and explaining to the deer next to him, "I don't exactly know why, but there's something about being near floatable soap that just gives me the willies."

What I gradually realized, though, was that writing about animals almost always requires two columns instead of one—the second to defend yourself from charges that you've been cruel to whichever animal you mentioned in the first. Animals tend to have more vehement adherents than, say, politicians. When Dan Quayle was vice-president, he had what I considered a particularly loyal group of followers; they were always writing me spirited defenses of him that rang with phrases like "He's probably not all that dumb anyway." But I would guess that any columnist who mentioned a description that was popular with the press during his tenure—that Dan Quayle had a stare reminiscent of a deer caught in headlights—received more mail from supporters of deer than supporters of the vice-president.

I got into what I consider a typical animal dispute in the summer of 1992 when I mentioned that we'd bought something called a deer whistle to keep deer from dashing in front of our car. The deer whistle, which consists of two little black plastic gizmos that you stick on your front bumper, was advertised as eighty percent effective, but we were having some difficulty making certain that it worked at all. In the first place, the whistle doesn't kick in until the car is going thirty miles an hour, according to the instructions, so to see if it's whistling someone would have to run in front of the car at that speed. This sounded dangerous, and frankly my wife said that she wasn't willing to try it. It wouldn't have done any good anyway. The whistle is pitched too high to be heard by a human being, particularly a human being who is running thirty miles an hour and presumably puffing like crazy.

Remonstrations arrived promptly from a woman in the state of Washington. She said that by making light of deer whistles, I had endangered readers of my column, not to speak of the general deer population. According to her way of thinking, readers who had been jollied into not taking the prospect of deer–car crashes seriously would put aside any plans they might have had to install deer whistles. Unwhistled-at deer would dash in front of their cars, and I would have the ensuing impact on my conscience—which, as the letter writer seemed to intuit, was already sorely overburdened.

At first I was reminded of the hummingbird incident—another one of my forays into the animal kingdom which resulted in a scolding. In a 1987 column based on learning that a hummingbird weighs as much as a quarter, I mentioned that my wife had expressed some concern about how one would go about weighing a hummingbird, and that I, trying to put her mind at ease, had said the method was similar to the one we've seen used on those nature programs that show scientists dropping wildebeests in their tracks with harmless stun-darts. In this case, I explained, the dart would be about half the size of a common straight pin. "It's surprisingly easy to hit a hummingbird with a tiny dart," I told my wife. "The difficult part is slapping him gently on the cheeks later to bring him around." No sooner had the column appeared than an enraged reader wrote in, attacking me for inspiring people all over the country to stick pins and needles into birds. I had to write a second column, which began, "I'm going to explain this whole thing in just a second, but right now please just do what I say: If any of you are sticking pins or needles into birds, stop it immediately. Don't ask any questions. Just stop."

Upon reflection, though, I realized that the criticism of the hummingbird column had been rooted in my failure to include some sort of warning—something like "Just joking, folks" or maybe even "Kids, don't try this one at home." A complaint on those grounds was easy enough to answer by the defense I have customarily made to anyone who objects to what appears in my column: you were not meant to take anything I write seriously. But that defense was useless against the deer-whistle advocate from Washington. Not being serious was precisely what I was being charged with.

She thought my observations about deer whistles were silly—I wouldn't argue strenuously with that view myself—but her criticism went beyond that. She thought they were tossed off irresponsibly, maybe even in reckless disregard of the consequences. In our litigious society, the logical end of that way of thinking is apparent: she was implying that if someone who has both read my column and failed to purchase a deer whistle hits a deer, I am liable. And me without a penny's worth of scoffing coverage!

If I am liable for the consequences of readers not taking deer whistles seriously, how about some of the other phenomena of American life that I have treated as jokes? The subject of the Reagan Administration leaps to mind.

I can imagine the case presented by the plaintiff's lawyer. Here was a president—a president who campaigned as someone resolutely opposed to deficit financing—cheerfully following policies that put more red ink on the books than all the presidents who preceded him combined. And what did the defendant do? He made jokes about how said president seemed to be under the impression that Polaris was a denture cleanser.

The plaintiff, who now understands that his grandchildren will be burdened with crippling debt, is asking compensation for the pain and suffering such a realization entails, and for a whiplash injury he suffered while trying to avoid a deer on the Merritt Parkway.

Thinking back on the subjects I may have been guilty of not taking seriously is disquieting: seat belts for dogs, grunge, the publishing industry, Renaissance Weekend, overpaid CEOs, the Iowa caucuses, the Senate Judiciary Committee. The list goes on and on.

The only defense I can think of is one that I learned from all the rich and powerful Wall Street figures accused a few years ago of insider trading: point the finger at friends and colleagues. You didn't take the Senate Judiciary Committee seriously enough to sweep all of those suits out of office? It must have been because of that hilarious Dave Barry column on the Anita Hill hearings. You thought the Reagan Administration was just silly instead of dangerous? It was Buchwald's fault, or maybe Russell Baker's. Not mine. I was writing mostly about animals.

March 26, 1990

Last month I read an Associated Press item about a man in Adams, Massachusetts, who, having bought the apartment building where his seventy-four-year-old grandmother has lived for ten years, raised her monthly rent from $96 to $400. She says that she can't afford to pay $400, because her income, from Social Security, is only $500. Also, she is a double amputee; in the newspaper that I saw—the *Daily Hampshire Gazette*, of Northampton, Massachusetts—the AP item was accompanied by a picture of her sitting in a wheelchair. You have to say this about the grandson, just for a start: this man has a public relations problem.

It's easy to imagine what the response might have been the first time he walked into his local tavern after the newspaper story appeared. The tavern is jammed, but it becomes absolutely still as he enters. He orders a beer. The sound of the bottle being set on the bar echoes in the silence. The grandson starts drinking the beer. Nobody says anything. He allows himself to entertain the ridiculous hope that nobody is ever going to say anything. Finally, Bugs Magowan, a regular, announces, as if to nobody in particular, "I don't see why he didn't just wheel her out in the hall and push her down the stairs."

"Like Richard Widmark in *Kiss of Death*," says Jack Bondoni, the local movie buff, and gives a pretty fair imitation of the legendary cackle that came from Widmark as he pushed the old woman in the wheelchair down the stairs. A lot of people begin trying the Widmark cackle. Somebody at the bar yells, "Why don't you just shut off the old bat's water on her birthday, guy? What are you, some kind of wimp or something?" Someone else, using the tune of "Bye, Bye, Blackbird," sings a song called "Bye, Bye, Grannie."

But let's look at the grandson's side. According to his lawyer, the grandson paid $125,000 for the four-unit apartment building and can't afford to meet his mortgage payments and make needed repairs unless he raises the rent. The lawyer says that the grandma and most of the other tenants are paying only a quarter of the market value rent, and a man from the Berkshire Regional Housing Authority who is trying to mediate the dispute confirms that $400 is "in line with the market." All that makes you see the situation in a different light. On the other hand, you still have to wonder if the leaders of those newly liberated Eastern European countries who talk about the joys lying before them once they adopt a "market economy" ever happen to see the *Daily Hampshire Gazette* of Northampton, Massachusetts.

The Eastern Europeans might be shocked at first by the Adams story, but one of those instructors in capitalism we've sent over there to help them with the transition from state economic control should be able to point out in the situation a firm principle of American business that is simply obscured a bit by the emotional reaction some people have to the prospect of someone's tossing his impoverished and crippled old grandma out on the street. The principle is this: the piper must be paid, and the customer must be the one who pays him.

Failure to understand this principle is why some Americans get exercised every time the oil companies respond to an oil spill by raising prices. To explain to lay-men how the piper principle works in oil spills, I've taken to using a simple example. Let's say you go to a restaurant and order the split-pea soup. Eventually the waiter comes out of the kitchen bearing a huge, steaming bowl of soup, but just as he gets to your table he trips and dumps the entire bowl of soup in your lap. Well, you're going to have to pay more. It stands to reason.

Think of the expenses involved. They're going to need paper towels to try to do some temporary damage control on your trousers. The waiter is going to have to spend some time at that, and at traveling back and forth into the kitchen. The busboy is going to have to be out there with a mop. Do you have any idea what a busboy gets paid these days?

Precisely the same principle applies in an oil spill. So, naturally, the price of whichever sort of oil is in-volved—let's say heating oil—goes up. The piper must be paid. Some ask what will happen to people on limited incomes—older people, say, even grandmothers—who can't afford to maintain their homes if they have to pay more for heating. We know the answer to that: Bye, bye, Grannie.

A NEW ARRIVAL

April 23, 1990

Nobody asked me what I thought we should call the new area code New York is expecting. Maybe the telephone people assumed that I was some sort of smart aleck who would have said "Kimberly" or "Jason." Maybe they thought that I simply wouldn't care. ("How can you bother me with area codes this soon after Earth Day? Let's talk stratospheric ozone depletion!") Maybe they figured me for the kind of troublemaker who would have pushed for an area code that wasn't compatible with the area codes we already have—something like 7 or 5,689. Wrong. I would have given the matter some serious thought. Also, I would have felt included.

As it is, I don't feel included at all. One day I just opened up the newspaper and read that New York was expecting a third area code. It is to be called 917. I couldn't tell from the article exactly who decided to call it 917—although mention was made of having applied for a new area code to something called the North American Dialing Plan, which sounds to me more like a process than an organization. ("No, your plan for dialing the first two digits with your big toe is impractical. What you ought to use is the North American Dialing Plan, which calls for taking the index finger . . .")

For all we know, 917 was decided on by the same telephone bureaucrat who named our last new area code

718—someone I have always thought of as the Far Away Man. The Far Away Man likes area codes that are numerically close but geographically far away. I have always thought, for instance, that 718, which is now the area code for Brooklyn and Queens and Staten Island, was chosen for its numerical proximity to 818, the area code for the San Fernando Valley.

A one-digit difference of three thousand miles is just the sort of spread that the Far Away Man likes. He figures that a bad hangover or simple carelessness is often good for a one-digit dialing error. He likes the idea of someone in the New Jersey suburbs picking up the phone first thing Sunday morning to make his weekly call to his dear old mother back in Brooklyn and finding himself in conversation with a young woman who lives in Canoga Park, California, and is not terribly happy about being awakened at six A.M. by a strange man who insists on telling her how much he misses her lasagna.

The way I imagine it, the Far Away Man listens in on some of these conversations, just to make sure that everyone is far enough away. At the end of his day at the office, he goes home, sits down at the dinner table with his family, and relates some of the best conversations to his wife, the Far Away Woman.

"That's very interesting, dear," the Far Away Woman says absently, as the Far Away Man tells her about a Vietnamese woman in Los Angeles who was trying to call her cousin in nearby Garden Grove and got one of those urban cowboy bars near Houston. Meanwhile, the Far Away Woman glances over to make sure that little 514 is eating his vegetables. Then she tells 802 to take his elbows off the table.

The last time New York got a new area code, I wanted to call it 093. My wife thought that was a terrible idea. "Area codes don't begin with zero, and they always have one or zero as the middle digit," she said. "Zero-nine-three doesn't even sound like an area code."

"Exactly!" I said. "This would be like naming somebody Montana or Shoe. It's hip, the girls go for it, and people never forget it."

Nobody paid any attention to me. The new area code was called 718. The people who were assigned 718— the people in Brooklyn and Queens and Staten Island— hated it. They thought that being 718 while all of Manhattan was 212 made them sound like second-class citizens instead of like people who make great lasagna.

So now the New York State Public Service Commission says it's going to seek public comments about which telephones to assign to the new area code. That, the commissioners figure, is going to make us feel included: the baby has already been named Nigel but we get to decide the color of the crib. One idea the Public Service Commission is considering is what's called an "overlay"—assigning the new area code not to some specific territory but to, say, all cellular phones. It seems odd to assign an area code to phones whose entire purpose is that they don't have to be in any particular area. Who would think of such a thing? I know. The Far Away Man.

June 11, 1990
It makes me sad to report that Minnesota, one of my favorite states, seems to have fallen into the hands of the rubes. But the evidence has to be faced. As the old Minnesota folk saying goes, "If the tobacco juice shatters into sharp little pieces when it hits the sidewalk, you better believe it's cold out."

Ironically, Minnesota had been gaining a reputation as a particularly sophisticated state—the final badge of sophistication being, of course, the ability to laugh at yourself. In the seventies, Dick Guindon, then the editorial cartoonist for the *Minneapolis Tribune*, attracted a great following in the state by making fun of its impossibly long winters. ("He seemed depressed because his car wouldn't start," a tow-truck driver is telling two cops as he nods toward a body in the slush. "And before I could stop him he had attached my jumper cables to his wet socks.")

Minnesota, of course, wasn't the only midwestern state trying to show this sort of sophistication. When someone suggested that the Wisconsin license plate motto ("America's Dairyland") should be changed to something more grandiose, on the order of New York's ("The Empire State") or New Hampshire's ("Live Free or Die"), someone suggested "Eat Cheese or Die." By that time, Milwaukee Brewer fans were already referring to themselves as Cheeseheads and showing up at games wearing hats in the shape of a wedge of the best Wisconsin cheddar. In other words, people from Wisconsin had savoir-faire.

But Minnesota had an unsurmountable lead, thanks partly to Garrison Keillor and "The Prairie Home Companion." You know a midwestern state is sophisticated when it takes pride in a national radio show that spreads the word on Minnesota gourmet specialties like hamburger hot dish and has features like "How to Talk Minnesotan."

This was going on, you have to remember, at a time when some midwestern cities (including, alas, Kansas City, my sainted hometown) were still controlled by boosters suffering from a disease I had diagnosed as rubaphobia—not fear of rubes but fear of being thought of as a rube. There is one thing you can count on about a rubaphobiac, other than the fact that he is likely to bore you silly with talk of how the city absolutely must have a world-class this and a major-league that: he is, in his heart of hearts, a rube. He would have his fingernails pulled out before he admitted he had ever heard of anything called hamburger hot dish.

There were setbacks in Minnesota, of course. Minneapolis built a domed stadium ("If we're going to be a world-class city, we need a real major-league stadium"), and domed stadiums are to rubaphobia what stretch limos are to the nouveau riche—a dead giveaway. But the mistakes were blotted out by the reassuring voice of Keillor talking about Lake Wobegon news such as the Sons of Knute decoy-carving project.

Everything seemed just fine until Mikhail Gorbachev breezed through. Suddenly people started talking about how Minnesota had become a major-league place. "I'd like to think we have put Lake Wobegon behind us," Al

Eisele, a Washington public relations man from Minnesota who helped arrange the Gorbachev stop, told the *New York Times*. "In some ways, Garrison Keillor did more damage to the image of Minnesota than Stalin did to the Soviet Union. We are more than a bunch of dumb Swedish farmers wandering around telling corny jokes."

Just for starters, as one of the Sons of Knute might say, Mr. Eisele, in the traditions of his trade, has the facts wrong. The farmers Keillor talks about are Norwegian, not Swedish, and there is nothing dumb about them. They would never think of comparing a funny storyteller to a dictator. Unlike a Washington public relations man, they would know that the trouble with Stalin was not that he created a bad image. The trouble was that he kept killing people.

Eisele told the *Times* that the Gorbachev visit helped to mold a world-class image for the state, and the governor seems to agree ("I think a lot of people all over the world now have some pretty good impressions of Minnesota"). I suspect that Minnesota's Norwegian farmers (Norwegian bachelor farmers, to quote Keillor exactly) aren't much interested in talk about being world-class. They know they're Minnesota-class, which ought to be good enough for anybody. They're not the ones who judge their own importance by the reflected glory of whichever celebrities—athletic or geopolitical—pass through the state. People who do that are, I'm afraid, rubes.

July 2, 1990

Do my ears deceive me, or can I actually hear the sounds of worms turning?

You say a turning worm makes no sound? Maybe not. But how about a chorus of turning worms? That's what's happening these days. Not long ago, for instance, some Russian reformer said that what the people really wanted was democracy and freedom and "Reaganism."

Reaganism! In Moscow, the world headquarters for gray bureaucrats and watery soup, the forces of enlightenment and progress are yearning for Reaganism! Here in the United States what seems to be the prevailing view of Reaganism, even among some conservative commentators, is that it was a disaster. Kevin Phillips, a noted thinker on the right who some years ago pointed out precisely how the Republicans could form a new majority in presidential politics, has just published a book saying that the excesses of wealth and greed and glitz in the Reagan years were so revolting to the general population that the pendulum is now likely to swing against conservatism.

So let's say that Phillips is correct once again, and that the pendulum keeps swinging. Here goes the pendulum here (some American politicians began to wonder whether some citizens should earn a hundred million dollars a year while some other citizens sleep in the street), and there goes the pendulum there (Russian legislators consider changing the name of St. Petersburg once more—to Adamsmithgrad).

The pendulum might well swing in a wider and wider arc. Over here, the Palm Springs mansion that the Reagans used to hang out in is taken over by the government and turned into a home for retired farmworkers from California hops cooperatives. When someone appears before the Moscow City Council to complain that his family of eight is getting turned out of its two-room rent-controlled apartment so private developers can turn half the building into a glitzy triplex for a billionaire LBO king, the city councilmen use an old Russian folk phrase that translates roughly into "That's the way the cookie crumbles, boychik."

You say such a thing is not possible? You say those boxy little Russian cars will never make decent stretch limos? You say if the worm turned that much, it would break its back?

In the first place, a worm doesn't have a back; that's the whole point of this worm-turning business. In the second place, this sort of thing is happening all over. Look at Quebec.

Yes, Quebec. In Quebec, people used to speak a sort of French that people in France dismissed as an archaic dialect of some other language, maybe Finnish. Now the French are having their own problems with French. They recently announced some spelling simplifications that were adopted, government officials acknowledged, partly because making the language easier to spell might encourage more people to study French instead of English. It's too late. One giveaway is that two of the words scheduled to be simplified by having their hyphens removed are "weekend" and "striptease"—English imports that the French once would never have admitted were in the language in the first place. Another giveaway is that a year or so ago, the Pasteur Institute in Paris had to take English rather than French names for its scientific journals because even scientists in supposedly French-speaking countries no longer submit articles in French.

And who submits articles in French? People in Quebec. That's right. Anyone who changed the name of a scientific journal from French to English in Quebec would probably be tossed in the slammer. The citizens of Quebec are so interested in speaking French that they may leave the Canadian federation just to do it. They're so strict about schoolchildren speaking French that at school assemblies you can't show films of English-speaking mimes. That's right. The mime has to be someone like Marcel Marceau, who is not speaking French, rather than a mime who is not speaking English.

All right, I made that up about mimes, but you get the idea. What I'm saying is that the worm is turning. People in France are arguing about whether there should be a hyphen in "weekend" and people in Quebec are arguing about whether it's O.K. to arrest someone for putting an English word like "weekend" on a sign, hyphen or no hyphen. It's only a matter of time before anybody who wants to speak real French will have to go to Quebec.

I can imagine rich Russians wanting to speak real French. Don't forget: before the worm turned the last time, rich Russians in nineteenth-century novels constantly spoke real French. The rich Russians jet off to Quebec on Aeroflot's special super-first-class champagne flight. They don't bother to stop in New York on the way. Nobody on the tour is interested in gray bureaucrats and watery soup.

July 9, 1990

So there I was, butchering a monkfish. As everyone knows, a monkfish is the ugliest creature God ever made.

I realize that those are fighting words among connoisseurs of the drastically unattractive. There are, for instance, people who sincerely believe that a catfish has got all other fish beat for ugliness. I'm here to tell you that compared to a monkfish the average catfish looks like Robert Redford.

In the Pacific Northwest there are people who think that the ugliest creature around is the giant clam they have out there called the geoduck. It's pronounced as if it were spelled gooeyduck, which adds to its unpleasant impression—although, as it happens, gooeyness is one of the few unattractive characteristics it doesn't possess. I won't try to tell you a geoduck is handsome. Its most striking feature is a clam neck that seems to be about the size of a baby elephant's trunk. Still, if I had to describe the appearance of a geoduck in a couple of words, I'd say "moderately disgusting." That's a long way from ugliness at the monkfish level.

The monkfish is also known by such names as goosefish, angler, and bellyfish. Calling it something else doesn't help. Its appearance still brings to mind that fine old American phrase, too little heard these days: "hit upside the head with an ugly stick."

The head, as it happens, is the ugliest part of a monkfish. It is huge—a lot bigger than the body. It is shaped sort of like a football that has been sideswiped by a Pontiac station wagon. It has, in the words of a fisherman I know, "all kinds of doodads hanging off it." In Nova Scotia, which is where I come in contact with monkfish, fishermen cut the heads off while still at sea. The stated reason for disposing of the head is that the fish plant won't buy it, since nobody has ever figured out a use for a monkfish head. (It doesn't keep long enough to be employed as a device you can threaten to show children if they don't quit fighting over the Nintendo.) I've never been able to escape the feeling, though, that fishermen cut off the head because they don't want anything that ugly on their boat. It makes them shiver.

If you were thinking that without the head a monkfish compares in pure natural beauty to, say, a snow leopard, forget it. The rest of a monkfish is plenty ugly. There is a skin that, by rights, ought to be on a geoduck or something that sounds equally gooey. Instead of the sort of bone structure a respectable fish has, the monkfish has something that reminds most people of a beef bone— although not in a way that makes them long for the open range. Covering the meat on either side of the bone there is a sort of membrane. Is the membrane disgusting? Try hard to think of a membrane you've really liked.

So there I was, butchering a monkfish. Why? Because in our part of Nova Scotia buying an unbutchered monkfish off a fishing boat is the only way you can get a monkfish, and monkfish, like catfish and geoducks, are absolutely delicious. Also, because I have always harbored a secret desire to have people say of me, "He's the sort of guy who can butcher a monkfish." If they did say that, of course, it might be misleading; I don't actually do many other things that are like butchering a monkfish.

On the other hand, let's face it: how many things are there that are like butchering a monkfish? Don't forget the membrane.

Removing the membrane is my least favorite part of butchering a monkfish, although, as a veterinarian I know always says about ministering to a cow that has a badly upset stomach, "There's nothing about it that reminds me a whole lot of opening presents on Christmas morning." I keep thinking that there's some sort of membrane-removal shortcut I don't know about. I always listen to the noon radio show they have for farmers and fishermen in the hope that someday I'll hear some home economist say something like, "To get the pesky membrane off a monkfish, simply bury the fish in cornflakes for fifteen or twenty minutes, then wipe briskly with a dry cloth." So far, nobody on the show has discussed monkfish. Probably too ugly.

So there I am, with the membrane and the gooey skin and the beef bone. What am I thinking? Sometimes I'm thinking, "Well, at least it doesn't have the head on." Sometimes I'm thinking, "Don't forget how good this is going to taste." When none of that does any good, I'm thinking, "You're the sort of guy who can butcher a monkfish."

July 16, 1990

I wish I could report that letters from people who read my column on butchering a monkfish reflected the response I was hoping for: "Gee, I didn't realize you were the sort of guy who could butcher a monkfish." As it turned out, a lot of people just wanted to know if I have a favorite monkfish recipe. Naturally, that included G.J.D. of Cleveland, Ohio—the smart aleck who is always writing to ask me the name of the secretary of agriculture. (Still none of your beeswax, G.J.D.) His letter said, "Do you have a special recipe for monkfish or are you the sort of sickie who butchers a monkfish just for kicks or what?"

As a matter of fact, I do have a recipe for a splendid monkfish dish. Here's how special it is: it's the only dish I can make. I don't mean the only monkfish dish; I mean the only dish. It's from *Catalan Cuisine*, a book by Colman Andrews on the food of northeastern Spain. In Catalan, the dish is called Rap amb All Cremat. Sometimes I refer to it by its English name, Monkfish with Burnt Garlic, but not often.

I realize that there are those among you who are going to find it odd that the only dish of somebody who can make only one dish is something called Rap amb All Cremat rather than, say, scrambled eggs. Oddly enough, scrambled eggs used to be my only dish. Some years ago

I made scrambled eggs every morning for my daughters before they went off to school. During that time I was asked to contribute a recipe to a cookbook, and I sent in my scrambled eggs recipe. I called it Scrambled Eggs That Stick to the Pan Every Time. There isn't any Catalan for that. Here's the recipe:

Ingredients: Eggs. Milk, if you can find it (back behind the lettuce, hidden by the shadow of the Chinese takeout leftovers). Butter.

Burn the butter while looking for sandwich bread for lunch or discussing the riboflavin content of various cereals. Apologize to your daughters for your language. Put a little milk (if you can find it) with the eggs. Shove all that around in the pan until you remember that the toast is about to burn. Turn back to the eggs, which by this time have stuck to the pan. Serve with burnt toast and a wan smile.

One day my daughters refused to eat the scrambled eggs. They staged a sort of selective hunger strike. They said they had always hated my scrambled eggs and weren't going to eat them ever again.

Did I attempt to reassert my authority, the way the wardens in prison movies do when the convicts start beating on the dining hall tables with their spoons? Of course. "I should send you to bed without your supper," I said.

"It's only breakfast time, Daddy," the older one said. "And you can't send us to bed now. We have to go to school."

She had a point there. Also, if they never ate my scrambled eggs again, I'd never have to wash that sticky pan again.

In a few years I forgot how to make scrambled eggs. (No, M.R. of LaPorte, Indiana, it's not like riding a bike; you can forget.) A lot of people—my daughters not among them—suggested that I find another dish. Meat-

loaf was the dish most often mentioned. I cooked meatloaf for a while, but I gave it up. I couldn't get very
excited about the prospect of being described as "the sort
of guy who can cook meatloaf." What I'm saying is that
I had no inspiration.

Then I heard some actor on a talk show explaining
why, after a lifetime of being cast by Hollywood as the
macho adventurer, he had decided to play Ophelia in an
off-Broadway production of *Othello*: "I wanted to stretch
myself." I decided to stretch myself with Monkfish with
Burnt Garlic. (No, M.L.W. of Cedar Rapids, Iowa, you
don't really burn the garlic. You brown it and combine it
with nuts and fried bread and parsley and olive oil to
make a sort of roux that the Catalans call picada.) The
first time I made it, it took all day. There's really not a
whole lot about the technique you learn in mastering
scrambled eggs and meatloaf that will help you in cooking
Rap amb All Cremat.

It was a triumph. To tell you the truth, enough picada would make old copies of *National Geographic* taste
pretty good. Now I make my only dish at least once a
summer. I think people are beginning to think of me as
the sort of guy who can cook Rap amb All Cremat.

July 30, 1990

According to a German newspaper called the *Berliner Morgenpost,* the East German Secret Police had a spy planted as a waiter in the catering firm used by the West Berlin Senate. After the dishes were cleared away, the waiter-spy would dig out a "secret infrared device" and beam to his masters the dinner-table conversation of such important Western guests as President Ronald Reagan. Clever dogs! It made me wonder again how we managed to win the Cold War.

It's something I've been wondering about ever since the Berlin Wall got torn down and the Eastern Europeans booted out the commissars and the Soviet Parliament itself began to resemble the state legislature of Louisiana. Oh, I know we were the good guys and they were the bad guys, but that isn't always enough. Bad guys win all the time. Some of them get caught sooner or later for insider trading and tossed into the slammer; a lot of them don't.

Also, the same people who kept telling us that we were the good guys made the Communists sound invincible. Sure, we had a few secret agents poking around out there ourselves. But from what we were always being told, our secret agents were at a disadvantage precisely because of their innate decency. The Communist secret agents were said to be totally ruthless—and even more important, they were everywhere. They were cultural attachés, members of trade delegations, concierges, barbers, bootblacks. Now we're told that when President Reagan himself had dinner in Berlin he was waited on by a Communist spy—probably a Communist spy with a miniature recording device planted in the soup ladle.

I picture this waiter-spy as a thin, slightly supercilious man with a neatly trimmed beard—a man who, when he filled in at chic West Berlin restaurants on evenings the catering company didn't require his services, approached the customer's table and said, in a rather patronizing nasal whine, "My name is Heinrich. I'll be your waiter this evening." When he worked West Berlin Senate dinners, though, Heinrich would have refrained from correcting American diplomats on which fork to use, in order to protect his cover for the big opportunity: serving President Ronald Reagan. Think of what a Communist spy could learn by listening to President Reagan throughout an entire meal!

Oh. Now that I mention it, that's a good question. What exactly could a Communist spy learn from President Reagan? What did the Tower Commission on the Iran-contra scandal learn from President Reagan? What did those poor devils who tried to take President Reagan's deposition for Admiral Poindexter's trial learn from President Reagan? Certainly not enough to justify keeping someone with Heinrich's tastes on the payroll all of these years.

That started me thinking. What secrets did we have that were worth all the trouble all those Communist spies went to? Think of all the money and energy the Communists used up to get information from a lot of people who didn't know a whole lot to begin with—us. Supposedly, the greatest triumph of the Red spy network was when they bought our war codes from that entrepreneurial Navy family, but, as it turned out, there wasn't any war. Money down the drain.

Think of all those trade delegates to London who spent so much time and money trying to butter up secretaries in the Defense Ministry or watching to see who went in and out of the service entrance of the American Embassy disguised as the termite-control man. Maybe, now that we look back on it, those trade-delegation people would have been better off spending their time trading.

At the highest levels, the Reds' decision-making must have been confounded by this spy business. Shouldn't those factories in the Ukraine be retooled, comrade? We can't afford to retool factories when we've got half the shoeshine boys in Lisbon on the payroll. Can you make a decision on the energy question, comrade? Not when my in-box is piled high with lists of everything the West German Embassy in Lima sent to the laundry for the past eighteen months.

Consider Heinrich's big opportunity. He uses his expensive infrared device to report everything President Reagan said at dinner. The East Germans make a transcript and shift forty of their best men out of economic planning to work on a microanalysis. The transcript consists mainly of President Reagan's retelling the plot of an old Dana Andrews movie. After six months the analyzers remain baffled. They turn to the rest of the transcript—a story about that woman in California Reagan heard about who picks up her welfare check in a Cadillac. Meanwhile, economic planning is a mess. No wonder we won the Cold War.

TIME AND TIDE

August 13, 1990

Those of you who have been grumbling that you never learn anything from this column will be relieved to hear that the world's highest tides are in the Minas Basin at the end of the Bay of Fundy, in Nova Scotia. I've been there. Did I see the high tides? Well, now that you mention it, that's sort of complicated.

My wife and I certainly showed up in Parrsboro, N.S., eager to see what the Minas Basin people had to offer in the way of tides. But how, exactly, do you look at a high tide? If it's in, it just looks like water. If it's out, looking at it is like observing some guy who bills himself as the person who has lost the most weight of anyone in the greater Cleveland area: to make a go of it, he'd pretty much have to have a way to show you what he looked like as a fatty. I don't mean to imply that folks along the Minas Basin would say that a bunch of mudflats are under water at high tide if it weren't true, but you can't be too careful these days.

Usually, something that's the highest or deepest or biggest is easy to spot. If you go to Pittsburgh and you want to see the largest revolving door in the world, for instance, you just ask anyone where it is. Then you can stand in front of it and say things like, "Well, that's a big revolving door, all right," or "In Houston, we got a whole mess of revolving doors bigger'n that," or "I wonder if that fat guy in Cleveland could have fit in that revolving door."

But it takes six and a half hours for a tide to change from high to low or vice versa, and the difference between high and low is actually the attraction you're supposed to observe. I could envision us lined up with other tourists at some lookout point designated by the tourist commission as one of the best places to get a look at the highest tides in the world. The tide is just going out. In six and a half hours, we're going to see a dramatic difference. After about an hour, the man next to me says, "You folks from Indiana?"

"No," I say.

He nods his head, as if my answer made a certain amount of sense. After a while he says, "Used to have some cousins in Indiana. Unless it was Illinois."

I look at my watch. We've got five and a half hours to go. I try to keep in mind that the word the tourist commission keeps using for these tides is "dramatic."

My wife broke into this reverie. "It says in the brochure that at high tide on certain days we could look for a tidal bore," she said.

"Not on your life!" I said. I happened to know what the brochure meant by a tidal bore: it's the wave that can be formed when the tide in a place like the Minas Basin comes into a narrow river that is flowing toward the sea. But before I realized that, I occasionally passed signs on the highway in Nova Scotia that said TIDAL BORE, and I assumed they were warning motorists about the presence of someone lurking around there waiting to tell you a lot more about tides than you ever wanted to know.

Whenever I saw a TIDAL BORE sign, I jammed my foot on the accelerator. Even after the true meaning was explained to me, I couldn't get over the idea that a living, talking tidal bore was just waiting to tell me at great length about the connection of tides and the phases of the moon. I couldn't get over the idea that another sign down the road might say NUTRITIONAL EATING BORE. Then there would be a sign saying TRIP TO EUROPE BORE, and just off the road, half hidden by a clump of bushes, he'd be there, waiting. What's that in his hand? A carousel full of slides!

I wasn't about to look for a tidal bore, and it occurred to me that we had another problem: we had arrived at half-tide, meaning that seeing the extremes of high and low would require us to spend more than nine hours at the lookout, all the time denying that we were from Indiana.

We drove down to the shore and took a look at the water. "I think, in a manner of speaking, we've sort of seen it," I said to my wife. "It was interesting."

"Somehow, I don't feel it was very dramatic," she said.

"Someday," I promised, "I'll take you to see the biggest revolving door in the world."

September 10, 1990

Recently, while talking with some friends about the relative nobility of the great states in this union, I commented that if I had to name a state that seems to be a particularly decent and civilized and physically uplifting place to live, I would say Iowa. Not a week after that discussion, the preliminary figures of the 1990 census were published. The runner-up in the dismal contest to see which state was deserted by the highest percentage of its residents since the census of 1980 was Iowa, whose population shrank by five percent. I sometimes get the feeling that I am not marching in step with the American people.

I always knew I had a problem in that regard. For years, I have been aware of the shadow present if I happen to mention to my wife that some new magazine has emerged as the sort of publication I find myself looking forward to: the magazine in question is almost invariably about to fold. Too many times to count, I have finished some novelist's grand opus convinced that, as A. J. Liebling once said of Hamlin Garland, "the man couldn't write for free seeds," and then watched the book in question pole-vault to the top of the best-seller list. Political candidates who strike me as attractive and capable people of character are usually swamped at the polls. If my name had any recognition factor at all in a political advertisement, a subcontest in any election would be an effort by each candidate to persuade me that I should come out publicly for his or her opponent.

It might be comforting to pretend that my taste is simply more rarefied and sophisticated than that of the great mass of people necessary to elect a candidate or produce a best seller—a notion my high school teachers would find amusing—but as it happens, I also disagree consistently with the experts. Almost every year they seem to vote for the wrong Academy Award nominee and pass up the best-looking Miss America contestant. I don't know enough to be certain that they choose the wrong people to induct into, say, the National Academy of Science, but I have my suspicions.

Iowa's shrinkage is just one more example. Why, I kept asking myself, would people leave such a place? Yes, of course, there are economic factors and employment factors. But could that account for a five percent reduction in population? Some people must have left out of a simple preference for living somewhere else. I see them as families that have moved from one of those perfect Iowa farmsteads—the ones surrounded by a grove of shade trees that can be seen from miles across the prairie—and now live in some dreary Sunbelt subdivision. What could they be thinking of?

I was one of the people who applauded during the movie *Field of Dreams* when one of the ghostly ballplayers asked if he was in heaven and Kevin Costner said, "No, this is Iowa." I was sympathetic to the objections from Iowa to a silly scene in that movie showing a public shouting match over banning a book, since neither shouting nor book banning is Iowa style. I once quoted an Iowa editor who said, when I asked him why his state had done so much more than any other for the Southeast Asian boat people, "Iowa has a better foreign policy than the United States."

After Jimmy Carter's operatives discovered the Iowa caucuses in 1975, I was not among those who complained that the caucuses were an awkward and unrepresentative way to start the presidential nominating contest. For my money, if the field needed a bit of winnowing, you couldn't have picked a better place to do it, although I was of course sorry to see the folks in Iowa pestered by all of those politicians.

Wait a minute! Maybe that explains it. During the ten years since the 1980 census, the Iowa caucuses have become more and more important, meaning a steadily increasing invasion of handshaking pols and pushy advance men and scrambling television crews—the whole bunch probably known in Iowa by some local slang phrase like "corn-tramplers." Maybe the thought of more and more of that every four years has driven a number of people from the state.

If so, the newspapers are carrying some good news: there haven't been any 1992 presidential candidates in Iowa yet. The Republican nomination is presumably Bush's for the asking, and not nearly as many Democratic corn-tramplers are expected this time around. I hope this news spreads to the Iowans who have left the state, particularly those who live in Sunbelt subdivisions: it's safe to go home now.

October 1, 1990
Castine, Maine, is a meticulously preserved old coastal
town where a lot of people put a date over the front door
to indicate when their house was built. No, I did not
mistake those numbers for house addresses and start asking why 1837 came between 1840 and 1858. You're not
dealing with some yahoo here.

My wife and I were being shown around Castine
early this autumn by an old friend I'll call Peter Davis,
who lives there. I was pleased to have Peter as a guide
because his own house in Castine was built in something
like 1786, so if we happened to come across some proud
homeowners raking the leaves or shining the brass in
front of, say, an 1845 house, we were in a position to cut
them dead.

People in Castine are so interested in local history
that there is actually a plaque—Peter later showed it to
us—on the spot where Madockawando, an Indian chief
with a particularly nasty temper, punished some slaves
for an escape attempt in 1692 by forcing them to eat their
own noses and ears before he had them burned at the
stake. I could imagine Madockawando peering closely at
the faces of his captives before their fate was announced
and saying, "I see you fellows brought your own lunch."
As historians sometimes say when their scholarly research

uncovers descriptions of the cruelty both sides were often guilty of in those harsh days, yech!

Feeling that I should chip in with something historically significant about the village in Nova Scotia where we had just spent a peaceful summer, I told Peter that in a remote and quiet cove not five miles from our house, the Royal Canadian Mounted Police last spring made the second largest seizure of hashish in the history of North America. It had a street value of four hundred million dollars, the authorities said, which is quite a haul even after you cut that figure in half.

"Why would you cut it in half?" Peter said.

"He cuts everything he hears in half," my wife said. "It started a long time ago. Whenever people started bragging about how many miles they got to a gallon, I could hear this murmuring next to me: 'Cut it in half, cut it in half.' "

"Well, not everything," I said. Years ago, I admitted that I did cut miles-per-gallon claims in half, and I generally do the same for boasts having to do with killings in the commodity market or, more recently, reports of cholesterol-count points dropped. That's also the policy I follow for real estate information from the sort of person who is constantly telling you how much his house is worth.

Considering the fact that a police spokesman, understandably proud of a drug seizure, may let his pride inflate his estimation of street value a bit, it does seem reasonable to divide whatever he says in half. I see this all as simple prudence, although my wife might use the word cynicism to describe it and—we might as well be honest here—there are those who have said that it reflects a view of humanity of the sort usually associated with a pawnbroker who's been in the business too long.

Still, I don't divide absolutely everything I hear in
half. "I accept some figures unadjusted," I said. "When
the man on the radio says that it's seventy-four degrees
at the airport, I don't automatically assume that it's
thirty-seven. Why should he lie about such a thing? Also,
I sometimes add rather than divide. These houses are a
good example. When I see a house that says it was built
in 1860, I figure it for somewhere between 1880 and the
turn of the century."

Why? There is, for example, the question of what
part of the house is being described. Once, when I was
at the Williamsburg restoration in Virginia, looking
through a building whose date of construction would
have impressed even the residents of Castine, Maine, I
asked one of the guides which part of the building was
original. "Everything below here," she said—a comment
I found most impressive until I realized that we were
standing on the ground floor. In other words, the original
part was a depression in the ground that had been identified as a foundation. So in a place like Castine, I just
add twenty or thirty years—a matter of simple prudence.

"That's a terrible thing to think about these people,"
my wife said. "The people in this town are so scrupu-
lously honest about history that they even put up a
plaque to tell that disgusting story about those poor people who had to eat their own noses."

"Noses and ears," I said.

"What?"

"Noses and ears," I repeated. "I think you may be
getting to the point where you cut everything you hear
in half."

SOUND POLICY

October 8, 1990

A while back, I read in the newspaper that a convenience store in Tillicum, Washington, had managed to rid its parking lot of teenage loiterers by installing a powerful loudspeaker and using it to play the sort of music ordinarily heard in elevators—effectively adapting the method used by those high-pitched electronic whines that are supposed to drive away mosquitoes. Not long after that, I read that more and more states have banned paddling in the schools, leaving open the question of what form of discipline to use instead. Then I put those two stories together for a jackpot educational idea: punish those little spitballers with a stiff dose of Mantovani.

A lot of people who have teenage children probably responded to the parking lot story as if it were the screenplay of a Hollywood film they had been fantasizing about for years: *Revenge of the Grownups*. They could envision, in the movie's opening scene, a parking lot that is filled with teenage loiterers, many of them staggering under the weight of their boom boxes. A grownup who parks there and walks toward the 7-Eleven—hoping to get a bottle of milk, or at least to get away from the constant rock racket in his own house for a while—is met with sneers and taunts and sarcastic references to Bing Crosby. As he stands waiting to pay for his milk, an idea comes to him. Within a couple of days the loudspeakers are set up and the first easy-listening tape has started. The teenage loiterers flee the parking lot, holding their ears and shouting things like "Arghh."

The word spreads. Grownups start showing up at the store bearing old LPs with titles like "Music for Romantic Dining." As a promotion, the 7-Eleven starts having special evenings, when the parking lot d.j. plays nothing but, say, the theme song from *Gone with the Wind* over and over again. The parking lot is now perfectly safe for grownups. In fact, a number of them start cruising the place on Friday nights. They ride around slowly in their clunky station wagons, exchanging greetings like "Hey, what's cookin'?"

That was not, of course, the way I responded. I filed away the story about the Tillicum 7-Eleven, thinking that someday I might be able to make use of it in a way beneficial to society. And sure enough, along came the problem of how to keep control of these little tykes if you're not allowed to whale the tar out of them. The article I read mentioned the possibility of replacing the paddling with after-school detention. From there it was only one step to after-school detention with Perry Como.

And from there it is only one more step to after-school detention with the momspeak tape. That is a tape produced by combining all of the things mothers say that most annoy their children. I suspect the 7-Eleven people had this tape in reserve in case the elevator music didn't work—their H-bomb.

As I see it, the offending spitballer is forced to sit in a plain room, furnished with a simple desk, a chair, and some posters of Dinah Shore and the Mills Brothers. A monitor outside the room flips a switch and the momspeak tape comes out into the room from loudspeakers high on the walls: "If I've told you once, I've told you a thousand times . . . I can't for the life of me understand why you have to play that music so loud . . . Do you have any idea what time it is? . . . Money doesn't grow on trees . . ." The spitballer, knowing that the punishment for a second offense is the dadspeak tape, vows to behave.

But what if even the momspeak tape proves to be unnecessary? What if some of those being punished with square sounds—who, unlike the loiterers at 7-Eleven, cannot simply flee—discover to their amazement after fifteen or twenty minutes that they rather like elevator music? What if they persuade some of their peers to give Guy Lombardo a chance? What if teenagers who carry boom boxes start using them to play tapes of the Lucky Strike Hit Parade? They get rid of their torn blue jeans and dangling earrings and start dressing in letter-sweaters and well-kept saddle shoes. The 7-Eleven announces that they're welcome back, although many would prefer to stay home and listen to Mantovani records with Mom or help Dad in the workshop with his World War I biplane models. Pretty soon the entire country is transformed. Nobody thinks to thank me for being such a careful reader of the newspapers.

October 15, 1990

Even though you may already be feeling just a little bit nervous geopolitically, I believe it's my duty to inform you that two people pretty important to the stability of the post-Cold War world—Stanislav S. Shatalin, the architect of the plan that will attempt to transform the Soviet Union into a market economy, and Fahd ibn Abdul Aziz, the king of Saudi Arabia—are in the habit of making their decisions only after consultation with astrologers. Does that make you feel any better? I didn't think so.

At this point, I would guess, you're trying to interpret this piece of news in a way that is not completely terrifying. You're telling yourself that basing a decision on astrology might not be as nutty as it sounds. You're reminding yourself that, after all, a president of the United States, Ronald Reagan, made some of his decisions after consultations with Nancy Reagan's astrologer. You're thinking of some of Ronald Reagan's decisions. Does that make you feel any better? I didn't think so.

Now you're thinking that maybe these two important people do not really consult astrologers. You're thinking that all this may be one of those little jokes of mine that you often find so irritating. Alas, this is not one of my little jokes. I read about Stanislav S. Shatalin's devotion to astrology in the *New York Times*. *Time* magazine reported King Fahd's dependence on the stars in a biographical piece that also included the information that the king, back in his playboy days, may once have gambled away a million dollars during a single weekend in Monte Carlo.

Does that business about losing a million in Monte Carlo make you feel any better about the efficacy of astrology? I didn't think so. Of course, it's possible that the king didn't consult his astrologer before he decided that the thing to do was to put ten grand a spin on number nineteen until it hit, no matter how long it took. Maybe the astrologer was off on a dirty weekend himself. Even if the king did consult his astrologer, maybe he's changed astrologers since then. Maybe he's switched to Nancy Reagan's astrologer ("The planets are perfect for trading arms for hostages and saying you didn't"). Feel better?

Well, you're saying, as you try to avoid contemplating the effect on your life if the Soviet economy collapses and Saudi Arabia does something truly wacky in the Gulf, it's not as if we absolutely up-to-date Americans don't base political decisions on some pretty dubious methods of predicting events ourselves—campaign polls, for instance.

True. A while back, some polltakers predicting how the Democratic gubernatorial primary in Massachusetts would come out agreed that the big loser, by a landslide twenty points, would be Boston University President John Silber, who is sometimes described as a candid iconoclast by people who are trying to be polite and as a bigot and a bully by people who aren't. In fact, Silber won by ten points—meaning that the polltakers, working in a discipline that is always described as having a margin of error of plus or minus three points, were off by thirty points. An astrologer probably couldn't have done much worse than that by attempting to predict the election results according to whether or not Jupiter was lined up with Worcester and Route 128 on the morning of the birth of Silber's barber.

The problem, of course, is that the people who are asked questions by polltakers are likely to lie. They're afraid that if they tell the polltaker they're going to vote for Silber, the polltaker will think that what they really mean is that they feel better about some of the vicious things they believe themselves if an important university president is saying the same things in public.

What people who believe in astrology don't understand is that the stars don't always tell the truth either. That's one reason the margin of error in astrology is plus or minus one hundred percent. Another reason is that the stars are even harder to read than polls: if you don't get the angle just right, what looks like Worcester may actually be Akron, Ohio.

Also, every sort of prediction business is chancy because nobody knows The Plan. An agnostic acquaintance of mine who has become exasperated with the Arabs during the latest difficulties told me last week that if there were a divine power, all of the world's oil supply would be under Denmark. But another possibility is that there is a divine power and He likes little jokes. Does that make you feel any better?

October 22, 1990

Just as the way to get a bank loan is to prove you don't need it, the way to sell a book is to have it appear on the best-seller list. A while back, the *Washington Post* revealed that the Gannett Foundation spent almost $40,000 of its tax-free money buying copies of a book by its chairman, Al Neuharth, in an effort to finagle it onto the list.

What Neuharth's boys were up to seemed only the latest in a series of developments designed to depress those ink-stained wretches who try to make a living writing books. Last year we were told that House Speaker Jim Wright got a royalty of 55 percent from his publisher. Then we learned that Congressman Newt Gingrich, the point man for the wacko battalions, was given $100,000 for book promotion by his friends and supporters. Now this.

No, now this and more. A month or so after the *Post* revealed that the Gannett Foundation had quietly furnished funds to editors of Gannett newspapers around the country and instructed them to buy Neuharth's book in the bookstores sampled by the best-seller list, it was announced that Ivana Trump is getting $3 million to publish two novels that she will not be required to write.

It's easy to imagine droves of writers crying in their beer (they drink a lot of beer, which is another problem) and lamenting the hard knocks upside the head that fate has dealt them: Why can't I find a publisher who gives a royalty of 55 percent? Why don't any of my friends want to chip in for my promotion budget? Why don't I have a foundation to help me cheat my way onto the best-seller list? Why can't somebody write my books for me and just leave me to collect the royalties in peace?

According to USA Today, Neuharth, the former CEO of the Gannett newspaper chain, "laughed off" the Post's story—always a mistake, I think, for someone with no humor—and the Gannett Foundation said it had simply wanted to buy some books for its educational mission. Since the foundation could have bought books at a 50 percent author's discount directly from the publisher rather than having stand-ins buy them at full price in selected bookstores, that left the impression that one of its educational functions is to train editors to stand in line at the cash register and ask for gift wrapping. Apparently not. The foundation executives said that what the foundation had in mind in buying the books and donating them to college libraries was that Neuharth offered "good practical advice on how to succeed in journalism and in life"—the advice being, if this incident is any guide, "Try to cheat, and then lie if you get caught."

Publishers seem to have absorbed part of that advice long ago, since they have for years routinely published books under the names of authors who didn't write them. Ivana Trump's books represent a departure only in that, because of the publicity machinery that has made her one of the last decade's premier examples of wretched excess, everyone knows she's not going to write them.

Also, of course, these are novels rather than nonfiction books—but only technically. Pocket Books is not giving Mrs. Trump $3 million to turn out an epic about a family of struggling farm laborers and a sensitive tale about a boy's coming of age in New Zealand. The idea will presumably be to provide yet another peek or two into the Trumps' glitz-lined trough with books that, unlike real novels, try to leave the impression that what is labeled fiction is actually true.

That would also give Mrs. Trump a shot at getting her side of the story in through a fictional character ("Supremely confident, Marvella Glump never corrected the rumors of extensive cosmetic surgery by revealing that, through an accident of genes, everyone in her family in Lithuania had found that aging constantly produced a firmer chin line").

I have no idea whether Neuharth actually wrote his book—some people who have read it assure me that the prose provides grim evidence that he might have—but for the next one he should consider hiring someone to write him something in the Ivana/Marvella mode. It could be about a former newspaper-chain CEO who's willing to take a chance that his book might make the best-seller list on its own merits. In other words, fiction.

THE ALICE TAX

October 29, 1990

The proposal by the House of Representatives to put a 10 percent tax surcharge on income over a million dollars a year—the proposal that so horrified the White House and caused grown senators to shake in their tasseled loafers—is seen by the tax specialists around our house as a considerably watered-down version of what we call the Alice Tax.

If George Bush had heard about the original Alice Tax—which has been proposed for years by my wife, Alice—he would have, to paraphrase the populist philosopher Bart Simpson, had a horseshoe. A true Alice Tax would probably inspire what the medical profession sometimes calls "harumph palpitations" in those senators who used the word "confiscatory" to describe a surcharge that would have brought the highest possible tax on incomes over a million dollars a year to 41 percent. To state the provisions of the Alice Tax simply, which is the only way Alice allows them to be stated, it calls for this: after a certain level of income, the government would simply take everything. When Alice says confiscatory, she means confiscatory.

The ruling principle of the Alice Tax is the concept of enoughness—a concept so foreign to the current American notions of capitalism that senators are able to see naked confiscation in a tax rate that people who made over a million a year in just about any other industrialized country in the world would consider piddling. Alice believes that at a certain point an annual income is simply more than anybody could possibly need for even a lavish style of living. She is willing to discuss what that point is. In her more flexible moments she is even willing to listen to arguments about which side of the line a style of living that includes, say, a large oceangoing boat should fall on. But she insists that there is such a thing as enough—a point of view that separates her from the United States Senate.

A congressman I saw on television being asked why the surcharge that passed in the House of Representatives was defeated in the Senate pointed out that a tremendous number of senators are millionaires—although, if I may be permitted to be fair for a change, they may not take in that amount each and every year. He was, in other words, arguing for the interpretation that the senators were loath to vote for the millionaire's tax not because their main bankrollers would be affected but because they themselves would be affected—that rare modern example of absolutely direct democracy.

To be fair once again—actually, I hate being fair twice in a row, but I feel I'm representing Alice to a certain extent here—the senators would argue that they were not protecting their own incomes but making certain that people vital to the economy were not robbed of their incentive. According to that reasoning, imposing a truly confiscatory tax after, say, an income of $10 million a year—a figure we can use for the sake of argument as long as Alice is not in the room—would mean that the entrepreneurial and highly motivated would stop their money-grubbing as soon as they reached that level, and thus rob the economy of the expansion their efforts bring.

In the first place, Alice would argue, they wouldn't stop. She would argue that the very fact that they devote their lives to trying to make more money than anybody could possibly use indicates that they behave that way not because they want more money but because they don't know any better. Also, the incentive argument assumes that what most of them do is economically beneficial to the public—an assumption that flies in the face of the past ten years of American history.

Let's take the case of Michael Milken, who made $550 million in 1987. If the Alice Tax kicked in at $10 million, he might have continued trying to rake in the booty anyway, meaning the treasury would be $540 million richer. But let's say he did call off his business dealings for the year when he reached an income of $10 million—which would have been on about January 6, according to my calculations. A lot of people who were laid off because merged or acquired corporations had to divert resources to pay debts might now be working. A lot of companies that may go under because of the burden of truly junky junk bonds might have survived. A lot of the felonies committed by Milken after January 6 might not have been committed. A lot of people who were cheated by those felonies might not have been cheated. I rest Alice's case.

CHECK HIM OUT

My wife and I went to Istanbul. A friend of ours I'll call Colette sent us there to check out her daughter's new boyfriend. That seems odd, I suppose, unless you yourself have daughters of serious-linkage age who live far from home. It didn't seem at all odd to us.

I hasten to say that we had already planned a trip to Istanbul before we got our assignment from Colette. I had some business there, although Colette informed me that it would have to take a back seat to the real mission. "You are in Istanbul to check out Juliet's boyfriend and return with a full report," she said. "If that leaves time for your other business, fine."

She said it rather like an intelligence officer in a World War II movie telling the American businessman who's about to leave for Zurich that he should carry on with his ordinary activities as well as he can while he tries to find out whether the Nazis are using Switzerland as a secret supply route for uranium.

In the movies the businessman usually begins by trying to turn down the intelligence officer who wants to recruit him ("After I bailed out of that burning B-17, colonel, I swore to my wife that I wouldn't make the mistake of risking my neck once too often, so you'll have to get yourself another boy"). But we accepted our assignment from Colette cheerfully. We've never bailed out of a burning B-17, but we've checked out plenty of boyfriends.

On the plane to Istanbul I told my wife that I had been looking forward to seeing Juliet even before we received our assignment and that I was certain that checking out the new boyfriend would present no problem to two checker-outers of our experience. "I didn't hear Colette say what this lad's doing in Turkey," I said. "Does he work at the embassy? Has he gone over there to study at the university?"

"He lives there," my wife said. "He's Turkish."

"Turkish!" I said. "Nobody said anything about his being Turkish. How are we supposed to check out a boyfriend who's Turkish?"

The boyfriends we've checked out have been American boyfriends. Our expertise is in American boyfriends. We know the field. We've established specific, easily applied standards. Take the question of earrings, for instance. We have what amounts to a body of case law on earrings. It goes back to when our own daughters were about the age the shampoo marketers call preteen. Out on a walk one day, I happened to pass a young man who was wearing four earrings in his left ear. When I got home, I said to my daughters, "I think you should know, for the future, that the answer to either one of you bringing home a guy with four earrings in his ear is a simple no. So don't even think about it."

"How about a guy with one earring?" my older daughter asked.

I considered that for a while. No parent wants to appear inflexible. "If he's enrolled in a fully accredited graduate or professional program, one earring is O.K.," I said.

I won't claim that the earring standard has not been adjusted over the years. The point is that there is a standard, and it can be applied easily to American boyfriends.

I know what I think about how an American boyfriend dresses and how he greets me ("Hiya, pops" is automatic grounds for not checking out) and what he's studying or what he does for a living. But a Turkish boyfriend! In Turkey, for all I know, four earrings in the left ear indicates membership in a student organization famous for producing eminent brain surgeons and distinguished supreme court justices.

"There's another problem," my wife said when I told her all of this. "Apparently his English is not perfect."

"We're checking him out in Turkish!" I said. "It's impossible. We should have turned down the assignment. We should have told Colette that we gave up this sort of thing after we had to bail out of a burning B-17."

My wife said we had to keep our promise to Colette. As soon as we could arrange it, we had dinner with Juliet and her boyfriend. I'll call him Ahmet. He spoke English a lot better than we had been led to expect. My wife and I liked him instantly. It was obvious that he would never have said "Hiya, pops" in any language. When we got back to the hotel after a lovely evening, I said, "Ahmet checks out."

My wife agreed. "You see, that wasn't so hard," she said. "It isn't necessary to have all those baselines and standards."

"Maybe not," I said. "Although you notice he wasn't wearing any earrings."

November 19, 1990

You may be wondering why I haven't gotten around to discussing the question of whether or not female reporters have a right to be in the locker rooms of the National Football League. As it happens, I'm still trying to deal with a news report of several weeks ago that a Japanese construction company barred a female reporter from a tunnel-completion ceremony because, in the words of the project supervisor, "the presence of women could anger the jealous Goddess of the Mountain." After that, I have to get to the issue of whether or not the Saudis should allow women to hold driver's licenses. In other words, I'm working up to this.

Before we proceed, I'd better state my position clearly on the general question of equality between the sexes. In previous comments on the public record, I have made it clear that I believe there to be no essential differences between men and women except that women tend to believe new slipcovers are needed in the spring and men have, deep in the chromosomes, an absolute compulsion to take out the garbage. That's where I stand.

You'd think someone with a position that forthright would have no patience at all for the argument by Japanese construction workers at the Sakazukiyama Tunnel that all women be banned from tunneling sites or with the response of the project supervisor, one Hatsuo Sato, who said of the banning of the female reporter, "I see nothing discriminatory in the action."

You would be absolutely right. My first response to the news from Japan was to say, "Nothing discriminatory! Give me a break, Hatsuo! How would you feel if you wanted to pop down to your local for a pick-me-up and you were banned because the proprietor said that the presence of a tunnel-construction project supervisor would make the God of *Sake* feel woozy? Also, even if there is a Goddess of the Mountain, what makes these construction guys think they know that the presence of women makes her jealous? Maybe she's the sort of goddess who likes the presence of women—the sort who enjoys kaffee-klatsches and pajama parties where they all get together and talk about how ratty the slipcovers are beginning to look."

Unfortunately I uttered my criticism of Hatsuo Sato's position in front of my friend Barton, who explained to me that I was failing to understand this matter in its cultural context. Barton always wants to understand everything in its cultural context. I can't tell you what a pain he is.

Let me give you an example. Several weeks ago, I returned from a short visit to Istanbul. Speaking within Barton's earshot of the increasing traffic problem in that otherwise noble metropolis, I said, "I mean this in the most constructive way and I wouldn't for a moment want to interfere in Turkish internal affairs, but it seems to me that it might help the traffic situation over there if they used lanes."

Barton told me that I was trying to impose an essentially Western notion on a Muslim nation that has one foot in Asia. I don't know how a country can have a foot anywhere, but that's the way Barton talks. Also, I don't know what the religion of a country has to do with traffic lanes. It's not as if it says in the Koran somewhere that cars should all move at the same time toward a narrow opening, like restless cattle moving toward the one hole in the corral fence.

Barton is the same way about the question of women not being permitted to drive in Saudi Arabia. What I suggested is that the Saudis could gradually phase in the right of women to drive. First they'd let women drive but Saudi men would be allowed to tell woman-driver jokes. Then, after a decent interval, the men would have to give up the woman-driver jokes. I think they could do it. I read somewhere that the Saudis managed to give up slavery twenty-eight years ago, so it's not as if they're that set in their ways.

Barton says that putting it in terms of woman-driver jokes is just another indication that I, as a Westerner, can't understand the situation. But I understand the situation perfectly. A Saudi woman wants to go out and comparison-shop slipcover fabrics. Her husband says the slipcovers they've got are practically brand-new. So she tells him to empty the garbage. While he's out there, she jumps in the car and is about to go downtown to the fabric store. Then she remembers: she's not allowed to drive. It doesn't have anything to do with the cultural context. It's against nature.

November 26, 1990
The fact that Ronald Reagan's memoirs came out just about the time that the singers of Milli Vanilli were exposed as not having done the singing on their album can be used to support the historical theory known to scholars as the Inevitable Confluence of Turkeys. The fact that Rob Pilatus and Fab Morvan of Milli Vanilli had their Grammy taken away while the ghostwriter and editors who put a number of Ronald Reagan's tired fantasies into complete sentences continue to think of themselves as respectable practitioners of a noble calling is yet another in a series of indications that the world of rock music has higher ethical standards than the publishing industry.

As Christopher Hitchens pointed out in *The Nation*, the Reagan turkey contains any number of statements and implications about Reagan's life and his presidency that have been disproved in the public press over and over again. While Reagan may by now have actually convinced himself, for example, that he was among the returning G.I.s who fought the Second World War, Hitchens wonders about the culpability of editors and ghostwriters who consciously pass off a lot of this old bushwa as historical fact. Actually, he doesn't wonder much at all: he calls them "accomplices to a fraud."

The publisher of Reagan's memoirs, Simon and Schuster, is known as a publishing house with a particularly strong devotion to the cash register—the unkind in the industry occasionally refer to it as Simon's Shoe Store—but its policies in the practice of ghostwriting are common to the trade. It is not unusual even for people who like to refer to themselves as journalists—people who would presumably enjoy blowing the whistle on some luckless manufacturer who tried to pass off as American something assembled in Taiwan—to sign their names to books they didn't write a word of.

Some of these books carry no hint at all that they were ghostwritten—not even an acknowledgments paragraph from which a reader who knows the code can divine the name of the actual writer. (The Reagan book had one of those, although you'd think all concerned might have craved anonymity.) Publishers, unlike rock producers, are never exposed in the press for presenting someone as the author of a book he didn't write. In publishing, lip-synching is considered perfectly all right.

Several years ago, I had a chat with a man who ran a half-hour book program on radio, interviewing authors who came through his city on promotional tours. He started by asking what I thought about the old gripe among authors that during such tours they are often interviewed by people who haven't read their book. I said that it seems unreasonable to expect, say, a local TV anchor who may interview a different touring author every morning to read five books a week in addition to his other duties. Then the radio man turned to what was for him the real problem: authors who haven't read the book.

"Authors who haven't read the book?" I said. "I don't think I understand."

"Well, more and more books are ghostwritten," he said. "So if I say to the author I'm interviewing on the air, 'You write here at the beginning of chapter nine . . . ,' it may turn out that he doesn't know what I'm talking about because he has never read chapter nine. He's never read the book."

"Once again I'm made to feel naïve," I said.

"I really don't mind if they didn't write the book," said the radio man, an amiable sort if I ever heard one. "But if they're going to be interviewed on a book program, it seems to me they ought to read it. Just as a matter of professional courtesy."

I would agree. Some years ago, I suggested that the publishing industry might think of complying with basic standards of truth-in-packaging by including with the blurbs it often runs on book jackets ("Hendricks writes like an angel with steel in its guts") the relationship of the person praising the book to the person who (maybe) wrote it: "old college roommate," for instance, or "cousin" or "just a friend returning a favor." That suggestion, I regret to report, was not taken up by the industry. Here's a second chance. Each book could just carry a standard statement, similar to the standard disclaimer in novels about the characters being strictly fictional. It would say, "The publishers certify that the author of this book has read it."

This might be a good way for the publishing industry to start its climb toward the ethical standards of Milli Vanilli. Rob Pilatus and Fab Morvan, after all, would never have shown up on a tour without having heard the album. In fact, they knew it well enough to lip-synch it.

January 21, 1991

For years I've been complaining that anyone who attempts to comment in a satiric vein on events in this country finds it difficult to concoct a situation so bizarre that it may not actually come to pass while his article is on the presses. It's what I call being blindsided by the truth. Another example is at hand. In 1986, Congress passed a law making it illegal for a private citizen to own a machine gun, and the National Rifle Association has fought the law all the way to the Supreme Court. No, I did not make that up. The fact that you think I must have made it up reflects precisely the problem I'm talking about.

Try to look at this from the viewpoint of those of us who attempt to keep the wolf from the door by cobbling together small jokes about the happenings of the day. One of the few tools we have at our disposal is exaggeration. Let's say that the point is to make fun of the NRA's maniacal opposition to the slightest attempt at regulating weapons. A columnist with a small amount of imagination—and that is the amount most of us have— might well choose to illustrate that point by envisioning the NRA's response to a law banning machine guns.

He could imagine postcard campaigns to remind Congress that the intention of the framers of the Constitution was to make certain that every single citizen had a machine gun. He could describe full-page magazine ads in which distinguished citizens testify that, as lifetime members of the NRA, they would hate to see the day when criminals had access to deadly weapons but a decent American guy couldn't even go dove hunting with his machine gun.

But the poor jokemaker has been robbed of that exaggeration. It's already true. Is he supposed to up the ante by imagining the response of the NRA to a law that would provide for a cooling-off period before a teenager with a serious juvenile court record and a history of mental illness could walk out of the store with a mortar or an antitank gun? You say that's too silly? I would agree with you. On the other hand, maybe it's already true.

You want another example? No problem. Let's take the case of Nancy Reagan, who is known as someone so obsessively concerned with her husband's place in history that Ronald Reagan's place in history may be as the president whose wife was obsessively concerned with his place in history. Let's say there is a columnist somewhere who has finally run out of Sununu jokes and has taken a blood oath never to mention Dan Quayle. Needing a subject as deadline approaches, he decides to have a little fun at Mrs. Reagan's expense. Too late. According to a recent item in *Newsweek*, poor Ronald Reagan now has to haul himself around the talk-show circuit one more time because Nancy Reagan can't stand the fact that his volume of memoirs, *An American Life*, is being outsold by *Millie's Book*, the memoirs of the White House dog. *Newsweek* quotes a "Reagan insider" as saying, "The dog book has really gotten under her skin."

Wait! It's worse than that. Here's something that not even someone who earns his living making mean, underhanded remarks about decent public servants could concoct: the dog's book is better than Reagan's book. Compare the reviews. Millie wins. The problem is not simply the old actors' saw about the inevitability of being upstaged if you do a scene with a kid or a dog. Reagan's book is so clogged with patently untrue fantasies that some reviewers have suggested as a more appropriate title *An American Lie*. The dog has had no criticism of that kind. If there is a jokemaker somewhere who was planning to comment wryly on boring White House memoirs by contemplating the possibility that a president is put in the literary shade by another president's dog, he has missed his chance.

I should report, by the way, that the Supreme Court refused to hear the NRA challenge to the law banning private ownership of machine guns, leaving in place a ruling by the Fifth Circuit Court of Appeals that the law is constitutional. So, you're about to say, the real events that compete with the imaginations of the jokemakers are not quite as bizarre as I make them out to be: we do not, in fact, live in a country that permits private citizens to own machine guns. Wrong. Trying to put a good light on the decision, an NRA spokesman reminded reporters that the hundred thousand people who legally owned machine guns before 1986 are unaffected by the law. No kidding.

A TRADITIONAL FAMILY

February 4, 1991

I just found out that our family is no longer what the Census Bureau calls a traditional American family, and I want everyone to know that this is not our fault.

We now find ourselves included in the statistics that are used constantly to show the lamentable decline of the typical American household from something like Ozzie and Harriet and the kids to something like a bunch of kooks and hippies.

I want everyone to know right at the start that we are not kooks. Oh sure, we have our peculiarities, but we are not kooks. Also, we are not hippies. We have no children named Goodness. I am the first one to admit that reasonable people may differ on how to characterize a couple of my veteran sportcoats, and there may have been a remark or two passed in the neighborhood from time to time about the state of our front lawn. But no one has ever seriously suggested that we are hippies.

In fact, most people find us rather traditional. My wife and I have a marriage certificate, although I can't say I know exactly where to put my hands on it right at the moment. We have two children. We have a big meal at Christmas. We put on costumes at Halloween. (What about the fact that I always wear an ax murderer's mask on Halloween? That happens to be one of the peculiarities.) We make family decisions in the traditional American family way, which is to say the father is manipulated by the wife and the children. We lose a lot of socks in the wash. At our house, the dishes are done and the garbage is taken out regularly—after the glass and cans and other recyclable materials have been separated out. We're not talking about a commune here.

So why has the Census Bureau begun listing us with households that consist of, say, the ex-stepchild of someone's former marriage living with someone who is under the mistaken impression that she is the aunt of somebody or other? Because the official definition of a traditional American family is two parents and one or more children under age eighteen. Our younger daughter just turned nineteen. Is that our fault?

As it happens, I did everything in my power to keep her from turning nineteen. When our daughters were about two and five, I decided that they were at the perfect age, and I looked around for some sort of freezing process that might keep them there. I discovered that there was no such freezing process on the market. Assuming, in the traditional American way, that the technology would come along by and by, I renewed my investigation several times during their childhoods—they always seemed to be at the perfect age—but the freezing process never surfaced. Meanwhile, they kept getting older at what seemed to me a constantly accelerating rate. Before you could say "Zip up your jacket," the baby turned nineteen. What's a parent to do?

Ask for an easement. That's what a parent's to do. When I learned about the Census Bureau's definition of a traditional family—it was mentioned in an Associated Press story about how the latest census shows the traditional family declining at a more moderate pace than "the rapid and destabilizing rate" at which it declined between 1970 and 1980—it occurred to me that we could simply explain the situation to the Census Bureau and ask that an exception be made in our case.

I realize that the Census Bureau would probably want to send out an inspector. I would acknowledge to him that our daughters are more or less away from home, but remind him that we have been assured by more experienced parents that we can absolutely count on their return. I would take the position, in other words, that we are just as traditional as any American family, just slightly undermanned at the moment—like a hockey team that has a couple of guys in the penalty box but is still a presence on the ice. We could show the official our Christmas tree decorations and our Halloween costumes and a lot of single socks. We might, in the traditional American way, offer him a cup of coffee and a small bribe.

I haven't decided for sure to approach the Census Bureau. For one thing, someone might whisper in the inspector's ear that I have been heard to refer to my older daughter's room—the room where we now keep the exercise bike—as "the gym," and that might take some explaining. Also, I haven't discussed this matter with my wife. I would, of course, abide by her wishes. It's traditional.

February 18, 1991

If I ever had any doubts about whether history truly repeats itself—as opposed to just clearing its throat now and then—they were put to rest by reading a recent item in the *New York Times* about people buying geckos for cockroach control.

The last time I dealt with the subject of geckos as hired killers was 1971. Nixon was in the White House. The college-tuition daughter was three years old and thought all my jokes were funny. (Yes, I may have told her the one about why the chicken crossed the road. Yes, I may have left the impression that I made up that joke. What are children for?) The report in the *Times* that geckos are again popular made a believer out of me on the question of history being just as repetitious as my Uncle Harry. I now find myself glancing over my shoulder regularly, half expecting the jitterbug to boogie out from around the corner.

Geckos, I should explain to those who have somehow forgotten what I wrote about them in 1971, are small lizards that love to eat cockroaches. (As my Aunt Rosie says, there's no accounting for taste—an aphorism she sometimes uses to explain how she happened to marry my Uncle Harry.) In 1971, some people I knew had bought a gecko and set it loose in their apartment on the West Side of Manhattan with instructions to take no prisoners.

When I wrote about this situation at the time, I disguised the names of the gecko owners—I called them Ralph and Myrna Cole—so that they wouldn't be revealed as people whose apartment was, as my friend Jane's mother always puts it, "crawling with cockroaches."

You may remember my friend Jane from my account of what happened when she had reason to believe that a cockroach had climbed into her computer. I didn't mention her last name, in order to guard against the possibility that her mother, who lives in Sioux City, Iowa, would get the impression that Jane's apartment was crawling with cockroaches. (Jane's mother doesn't really live in Sioux City, Iowa; that's part of the disguise.) Having been reminded of geckos by the piece in the *Times*, I told Jane that the next time she sees a cockroach crawl into her computer, maybe the thing to do is to send a gecko in there after it. Jane told me that she is trying to forget the entire experience. She said that if I mention her in connection with this, she'd appreciate it if I referred to her as Blanche, just in case.

Anyway, when I read that geckos were back, I immediately thought of phoning the people I called Ralph and Myrna Cole to find out whether they still had their gecko. Of course, I wasn't certain that such a thing was possible, since I'm not right up to the minute on the lifespan of a gecko. Also, as I remembered it, the Coles hadn't been absolutely certain that they still had their gecko in 1971. Geckos are known to be terribly shy—the pet-shop people say this is a great advantage, since an owner is not likely to wake up and find himself eyeball to eyeball with one—and when I interviewed the Coles they hadn't seen theirs in weeks.

So maybe my phone call would find them in the midst of mourning their gecko or in the midst of looking under couches and behind cushions, still trying to find the little rascal. But this is the kind of tough phone call we reporters are trained to make. I picked up the phone. Then I realized that I didn't know who they were. It had been so long ago that I couldn't remember their real names.

"Maybe they were the Conrads," my wife said. "From the looks of the Conrads' apartment, I've always suspected that it's crawling with cockroaches."

"Not the Conrads," I said. "In 1971 the Conrads were still living in that commune in Vermont that gradually evolved into a shared summer house."

"Maybe the Johnsons," she said. "They were very trendy. If anteaters got fashionable, they'd buy an anteater."

"The Bartletts!" I said. That's not their real name, which I won't mention because what reminded me of them is that I've always thought Don Bartlett looks a little bit like an anteater.

"But the Bartletts have been divorced for years," my wife said.

"What a pity," I said. "This would have been a little milestone for them—the return of the gecko. Maybe they'll get together again."

"I don't think so," my wife said. "I think it finally occurred to Edna Bartlett that Don looks a bit like an anteater."

"You never can tell," I said. "History often repeats itself."

DOG-BARK DUET

February 25, 1991

It's true that Princess Gloria von Thurn und Taxis and I can both bark like a dog, but we have very little else in common. I just wanted to get that off my chest.

Apparently, the princess and her late husband, Prince Johannes von Thurn und Taxis, who died last December, managed to run through a couple of billion dollars (leaving only five hundred million or so) while hanging around with that gang of rich glitz-hounds and Eurotrash party-trotters and titled deadbeats that a friend of mine used to call "the useless tassel at the end of society." That's not my sort of thing at all.

Ordinarily I wouldn't have even said anything about any of this. I'm not the sort of person who sits around worrying about the possibility that somewhere someone might be comparing him to somebody in the Useless Tassel. ("No, I don't think he's much like the late King Farouk of Egypt, although if he doesn't start going light on the pasta he may get there one of these days. But there's something about him that puts you in mind of Princess Gloria von Thurn und Taxis.")

The only reason I'm mentioning this at all is that another friend of mind, Roy, sent me an article he had torn out of a slightly out-of-date *People* magazine about the Prince and Princess von Thurn und Taxis. After touching on some of the highlights of the life they led together—throwing a two-million-dollar costume ball; maintaining a fleet of twenty limousines plus a Harley-Davidson for the princess; indulging in the little jokes the prince so loved, like serving his guests vinegar-filled pralines or slipping a piranha into the aquarium of a collector of exotic fish—the *People* article said that the princess occasionally appeared on a Munich talk show "doing her famed impression of a barking dog." Roy circled that part and wrote next to it, "If you and she ever appear together, I would like to see it."

I should make it clear that before I gave any thought to myself I thought about Roy. I identify slightly out-of-date copies of *People* magazine with dentists' offices, and I hoped this wasn't an indication that Roy was having more trouble with his teeth. We happen to go to the same dentist—the healer we call Sweeney Todd, D.D.S., whose diagnoses always seem closely tied to his own cash-flow situation. Sweeney has been madly rearranging mouths ever since his wife spotted a beach house she craved on the Jersey shore.

In my own case, I have reason to believe that Sweeney is putting together a combination on the lower right—a root canal here, an extraction there—with a gold bridge in mind. He drills away with the single-mindedness of a New York real estate shark quietly accumulating a line of stores to be torn down for a particularly lucrative high-rise. If Roy was in for that sort of project, he could forget any dreams he might have had about owning a fleet of limos and a Harley.

I should also say that I appreciated Roy's kind words about my dog bark, which is my only first-rate animal imitation. Roy has been present when I've done my dog bark in public, and it's gratifying that he would like to see it again. There are, after all, people who think that one exposure to a well-executed dog-bark imitation is sufficient. In fact, I would put my own wife in that category.

Still, I was concerned. A couple of years ago, someone published a book portraying Picasso as an exceedingly unpleasant fellow, and my cousin Fred, the Wal-Mart assistant store manager and amateur watercolorist, was afraid everyone would think he is a brute just because he's a Sunday painter. His wife, my cousin Stephanie, offered to make a public statement that Fred never abused her ("Listen, I hardly ever see the guy"), but Fred said he was so upset that it was affecting his art.

Maybe some people are defending Princess Gloria Thurn und Taxis the way some people defended Picasso ("Listen, if her dog-bark imitation is brilliant, her personal life is simply irrelevant to the discussion of her as an artist"). I don't want to bark a duet with her anyway. I want to make it clear that I have never even known any royalty of any kind, unless you count a smooth dresser in my high school we always referred to as the Prince of Suave. Princess Gloria and I are simply not alike. In fact, since Sweeney Todd, D.D.S., had his last go at the lower right, I'm not even certain I can bark like a dog.

March 18, 1991

Around the first of the year, the *New York Times* published a list of geographical name changes that took place over the past decade—the change in 1984, for example, that transformed the Republic of Upper Volta into Burkina Faso—and I've been studying the list ever since. I may have lost interest in the names of the Bush Administration cabinet secretaries by now, but when it comes to geography, I like to be up to the minute.

As you must have realized, geography is my best subject. I've often mentioned how upset I get every time some survey-taker comes back with strong indications that many American high school students would probably identify Alabama as the capital of Chicago. If a survey-taker asked me to identify Alabama, I would not just identify it. I would name its capital. I would tell him the names of rivers that run through Alabama, plus their tributaries. If I happened to be in a show-offy mood, I would toss in major mineral resources.

The list in the *Times* was credited to Zoltán Grossman, Mapping Specialists Ltd. of Madison, Wisconsin (Madison is, of course, the state capital, and had a 1980 population of 178,180). I have no idea how the company is organized, but in my mind it exists as a man named Zoltán Grossman—a man with a cosmopolitan air and a slight Middle European accent and a feeling for geography so instinctive that the very mention of Burkina Faso causes him to mouth the word "Ouagadougou" (the capital) and maybe even the word "manganese" (the major mineral resource).

Going over the list, I sometimes carry on a sort of imaginary conversation with Zoltán Grossman. In my mind we are sitting at a sidewalk café in some unnamed European city—population, we both know, 864,362. I congratulate him on catching the change of Brunei to Brunei Darussalam, a change a lot of geography hounds missed, and I somehow work into that compliment a reminder of my observation some years ago that South Yemen was not, in fact, south of Yemen—an observation that I like to think may have had something to do with their eventual union. Grossman smiles, nods almost imperceptibly, and tips his cup of espresso to me in an ironic little salute.

Sometimes, in those conversations, I allow myself an occasional small complaint about how the list of name changes was presented. Although I appreciated being told that in 1986 the rivers in Burkina Faso that were formerly called the Black, Red, and White Volta rivers became the Mouhoun, Nzinon, and Nakanbe rivers, I tell Grossman, I would have appreciated it even more if I had been told whether this was in tribute to some Burkina Faso patriots ("General Nzinon is a loyal supporter of President Mouhoun") or simply a translation of the colonial names into some other language, perhaps the language of the Mossi, Burkina Faso's largest tribe ("If the general attacks on a mouhoun night, the Nakanbe will run nzinon with blood").

"Perhaps you're right," Grossman says. "And perhaps we should have offered the same sort of explanation concerning the change of the name of Greenland in 1982 to Kalaallitt Nunaat."

"Touché, Monsieur Grossman," I say. Grossman,

that sly devil, is obviously aware that in a column in 1987, a full five years after the official change, I referred to Kalaallitt Nunaat as Greenland—an embarrassing mistake that made me feel like some kalaallitt reporter who had just nunaated his first job.

In general, though, Grossman and I do not try to catch each other in errors. We sit for hours at the café, chewing over such questions as whether the presence of so many double letters in the Greenlandic language might mean that an appropriate place for the annual conference of the Twins Society would be the Kalaallitt Nunaat capital of Nuuk.

We might spend some time talking about how Cambodia changed to Kampuchea and then, before some of the atlas people could catch up, back to Cambodia again. We might speculate on the parliamentary debate that resulted in the Federation of St. Kitts–Nevis changing its name to the Federation of St. Kitts and Nevis. Were there, for instance, people known as Hyphenists and people known as Antihyphenists?

Grossman, as I imagine him, is constantly disappointed in the United States, his adopted home, where names hardly ever change. When he gets nostalgic, he talks of the time that Hot Springs, New Mexico, changed its name to Truth or Consequences, New Mexico, which was in 1950.

"Perhaps they'll change back someday," he sometimes says in a reflective moment.

"I'll believe it when I see it, Herr Grossman," I say. "I was raised in the Show-Me State—Missouri."

"Jefferson City," Grossman says quietly. "Zinc and lead."

March 25, 1991

I didn't think I needed any further confirmation of those lamentations we're always hearing about the dismal state of ignorance most Americans are in when it comes to science. After all, I'm one of the people they're talking about.

In fact, I've been straightforward about owning up to my own failings in this area. I admitted publicly that until recently I was under the impression that Orion was spelled O'Ryan, and had always found it puzzling that there was one constellation of Irish descent. I admitted publicly that for a long time I took it for granted that decaffeinated coffee was produced by a labor-intensive industry whose principal tool was tiny tweezers and whose principal environmental hazard was the accumulation of caffeine slagheaps so potent that a curious dog who sniffed at one would be awake for eight or ten years. What I'm saying is that I've never claimed to be a whiz at this stuff myself.

Still, even I was shocked by the latest evidence of scientific illiteracy—the results of a little survey I carried on myself. Here's how it worked. First, I reported in this column that I often take people who are visiting New York to see the Frog Mountains of Chinatown. (We all have our own ideas of the big sights.) Two restaurants I know of in Chinatown hold frogs in the sort of wall tanks that Chinese restaurants ordinarily use for the display of fish, and in both cases the frogs are so insistent on moving back from the glass and to the right that they climb up on one another to form small, squirmy piles in the corner—the so-called Frog Mountains of Chinatown.

In the course of talking about what a grand tourist sight a frog mountain can be, I mentioned that the visitors I take to Chinatown have varying theories about why the frogs move back and to the right—one theory being that all frogs are born in the same place, a pond in southern Indiana, and that these particular frogs, sensing what must be in store for a frog being held in a tank in a Chinese restaurant, are trying desperately to get back there.

That's silly. Even I knew that was silly. For one thing, it's common knowledge that southern Indiana doesn't have that many frogs. Also, even though the frogs in one restaurant seem to be trying to move toward southern Indiana, the frogs in the other restaurant are pointed more or less in the direction of Spartanburg, South Carolina.

I only mentioned that theory about the pond in Indiana in the hope that it would provoke people to offer better theories. I figured I would get a lot of letters that began, "You're thinking of eels all being born in the same place," and would then go on to tell me the real reason frogs are always so desperate to move back and to the right—something about whether frogs use the right or left side of their brains, maybe, or something about how all frogs are just naturally a little lopsided. This wasn't one of those dumb riddles; I really wanted to know.

Nobody sent any theories. Oh sure, I got the predictable letter from some cliché-monger telling me that frogs' legs taste just like chicken and the predictable letter from a frogs'-rights advocate who told me that anyone worth his salt would have smashed the wall-tank glass to liberate the imprisoned frogs. And yes, I got the predictable letter from some political nut telling me that the use of "frog" as a mildly derogatory term for Frenchman derives from the fact that when Frenchmen are frightened they tend to move back and toward the right—an example being the instant retreat and the formation of the fascist government in Vichy at the beginning of the Second World War.

But nobody told me why frogs move back and to the right. The only letter that contained what you might call a scientific theory said, "Anybody who ever for even a minute thought that caffeine was removed from coffee beans with tiny tweezers is a nitwit." No wonder the Japanese beat us to Nintendo.

May 13, 1991

Right at the start, let's clear up the question of whether I ever said that this country would be a lot better off if every single person who was in Au Bar in Palm Beach at 3 A.M. on a Good Friday—or any other morning—was deported to New Zealand.

What I really said was this: even though I would never be in favor of such a draconian measure, which would violate all of my most cherished beliefs about due process and civil liberties, I think it's interesting to speculate, strictly theoretically, about whether such a mass deportation would be a net gain for the society.

That's not saying the same thing. In the first place, it's important that this is only theoretical. In the second place, don't forget what I said about net gain: I'll admit that some people of value would be swept up when the Immigration and Naturalization Service authorities showed up at Au Bar and loaded everyone in paddy wagons whose drivers had strict instructions to go directly to the airport. I would guess, for instance, that a few innocent college kids on spring break in Florida might be there, simply because they are likely to wander into any saloon that has a light on at three in the morning.

These college kids wouldn't be there because they aspired to the hot Palm Beach bar scene of particularly drunken coupon-clippers and assorted Eurotrash. They might just want another beer. I'd hate to see them snatched up and, without even a chance to make a phone call or stop at home for a clean shirt, shipped off to some sheep farm three hundred miles from Auckland. There is also the matter of Senator Kennedy, apparently an Au Bar regular, whose departure would be, in the opinion of many, a loss for the Senate.

I have to admit that long before the incident in Palm Beach I often found myself engaged in idle speculation about mass deportation. At times I could imagine the INS cops showing up at some nightspot; that was particularly true when Studio 54 was in business. Sometimes I would organize the operation by what people did or what they owned. "Attention, attention," I would say, usually while in the shower. "Attention, all owners of stretch limousines. This is a recall. Not the car—you."

Toting up net gain is not difficult. In the case of Au Bar, you simply put on one side of the scales, say, these students (who could someday be productive citizens) plus Senator Kennedy's diligent work on the Senate Labor and Human Resources Committee. On the other side you put the drunken coupon-clippers and assorted Eurotrash. Then, strictly theoretically, you decide whether mass deportation would represent a net gain.

I hasten to say that this is not meant as a judgment on either the alleged attacker or the alleged victim in the incident that took place at the Kennedy house. I don't know which side of the scales either one of them would be on. Even if I did, I wouldn't follow the example of the *New York Times*, which decided that it owed its readers not only the name of the alleged victim but such details of her life as the fact that she had accumulated a number of traffic tickets and had a child out of wedlock and, according to an anonymous source, had "a little wild streak" in high school.

One problem with that approach, it seems to me, is that the *Times* may now feel it owes its readers a background piece on practically anyone who reports that he has been a victim of a crime—a mugging ("Although he is nearly six feet tall, Mr. Cranston has what several acquaintances of his describe as 'not a very purposeful walk' and in high school was, in the view of one classmate who did not wish to be identified, 'sort of a nerd' ") or even a burglary ("Mr. Molson acknowledged that when he and his wife were in high school together, her locker combination was an open secret in the junior class").

Also, the *Times* mentioned the alleged victim's name because NBC had done it, and NBC did it because a supermarket tabloid had done it. That sort of thing tends to lump all of us in the press together, which worries me, just in case there is ever a point at which people who have fantasies about mass deportation can make them come true. I can envision someone announcing, "Attention, all press people: stand in front of your doors for immediate pickup."

May 20, 1991

Parents who have been worried about their children being turned into mindless layabouts by rock-music lyrics will be relieved to hear that, according to the latest scientific studies, teenagers pay virtually no attention to the lyrics of rock songs. In other words, just what is turning these teenagers into mindless layabouts is still open to question.

I should also say, in the spirit of generational fairness, that there have been no studies so far to see what is turning so many parents into mindless layabouts. That is probably a much longer story.

According to an article I read in the *Washington Post*, one of the most thorough studies ever done on the impact of rock lyrics was recently completed by two psychologists from California State University at Fullerton, Jill Rosenbaum and Lorraine Prinsky. They found that most teenagers don't listen closely to the words of rock songs, don't catch a lot of what they do hear, and don't much care one way or the other. When the teenagers in the survey were asked why they listen to a rock song, "I want to listen to the words" finished dead last.

This information should change one of the standard discussions that parents and teenagers have about rock music—a discussion traditionally carried on in the family automobile at a time when the music blaring from a boom box in the back seat is loud enough to turn the windshield wipers on and off.

Parent (in a patient and mature tone): I can't imagine why you listen to that moronic garbage.

Teenager: Uhnnn.

Parent: It's just a lot of thugs making as much noise as they can.

Teenager: Nghh.

Parent: Half the time, you can't even make out the words to the song anyway.

Teenager: Actually, much more than half the time. But the latest study indicates that this makes no difference whatsoever in my enjoyment of this art form.

That's right. Teenagers don't care about the words. They listen to the lyrics of rock songs about as carefully as their parents listen to the lyrics of "The Star-Spangled Banner."

The California study found that the messages supposedly encoded in some rock songs—exhortations to become dope fiends and burn down cities and worship Satan and engage in hideous sexual excesses and leave the dinner table without being asked to be excused and that sort of thing—were lost on teenagers, even when the researchers furnished printouts of the lyrics for the teenagers to peruse. This is, of course, good news for parents and discouraging news for anybody who has put a lot of effort into trying to use rock lyrics to encourage teenagers to do wicked things.

Since teenagers don't listen carefully to the lyrics, they tend to form their opinion of what the song is about from the title. For instance, the Bruce Springsteen hit "Born in the USA" is described by the *Post* as having "in every verse explicit references to despair and disillusionment." But kids from fourth grade through college who were tested by researchers from the University of California at Los Angeles were mostly under the impression that "Born in the USA" was a patriotic song.

These results shouldn't surprise anybody. Most grownups don't get much past the title of anything, which is why title-writing is such an art. The military is particularly adept at titles. The invasion of Panama, for instance, was called Operation Just Cause. Think of what the public impression of that episode would have been if the Pentagon had chosen a name that would have been, in fact, much less subject to differences of opinion: Operation Tiny Country. Think of how the public view of the war in the Persian Gulf might have differed if our military effort to drive Iraqis from Kuwait had been called not Operation Desert Storm but Operation Restore Despot.

The results of these rock-lyrics studies seem to indicate that putting warning labels on rock records would only draw teenagers' attention to something they might otherwise ignore—sort of like marking the spines of innocent-looking novels, "Warning: This Book Has Some Good Parts."

The results also mean that concerned citizens would be wasting their time mounting a campaign to encourage songwriters to compose more uplifting lyrics. That's a shame. I was sort of looking forward to the forces of good coming up with a song that featured endless repetition of some lyric like "I wanna clean my room" or "I appreciate the great burden of responsibility my father carries and the sacrifices he's made on behalf of me and my siblings, and I have only the greatest respect for him." With the right tune, we now know, that might have made the charts, but nobody would have been listening anyway.

May 27, 1991

It's been more than two months since I read in the *Washington Post* that in Germany the government has to approve the name of your child. I think my response to the *Post* item has paralleled the stages people sometimes move through in response to a family catastrophe, beginning with denial and going on to anger. I now remember specifically that the first words I uttered upon reading the item were "Get serious!"

That's right. I thought it was a joke. For a moment it occurred to me that the entire edition of the *Washington Post* I was reading might be what we used to call at the college paper (usually on April Fools' Day) a yuk issue, and I turned back to the front page to see if it had headlines like GORBACHEV NEW HOST OF HOLLYWOOD SQUARES and SUNUNU SAID TO BE UNCERTAIN ON WHETHER TO REAPPOINT BUSH and HELMS DEFENDS PORN THEATER VISIT AS ''RESEARCH.''

But the front page was obviously real, and so was the story I had just read. In Germany, if the clerk in charge of such matters at your city hall doesn't approve of the name you propose to give your newborn baby, you have to name the baby something else. That's right: the clerk. The government says it's a question of the clerk protecting the child. If they tried that in this country, the question would be, Who's going to protect the clerk?

In Germany, on the other hand, there are all sorts of regulations like this that the citizenry docilely accepts—although the *Post* piece did report that a doctor in Düsseldorf recently went to court to challenge a law that makes it a crime to take a shower after ten in the evening. (I know what you're saying now. You're saying, "Get serious!" That means you're in the denial stage. I suggest that you go to your public library, look up the *Washington Post* for March 25, 1991, and turn to page A14. Then you can move on to anger.) Next time you're assured that we have a strong cultural unity with the countries of Western Europe, keep in mind that Germany has laws against taking a shower after 10 P.M.

In Germany, name clerks routinely turn down names that don't make it clear whether the child is a girl or a boy, for instance, or names that might sound unfamiliar to the other children at school or names that mean something odd in the language of a foreign country that the child in question will almost certainly never visit.

Let's say that you want to name your new son Leslie because you have reason to believe that your rich and essentially vicious Uncle Leslie would be so touched by such a gesture that he would leave you a bundle to see little Leslie through college. (I'm using American names because I don't want to irritate you with unfamiliar German names at a time when this thing has already put you in a bad mood.)

The clerk says absolutely not: little Leslie could be mistaken for a female. You say that if enough of Uncle Leslie's boodle is involved, you don't care if little Leslie could be mistaken for a parking meter. The clerk says no. You appeal to a court. The judge upholds the clerk. You get so mad that you take a shower at 10:15. You get arrested. Now this kid of yours has real problems: he doesn't have a name and one of his parents is in the clink.

I don't mean that I approve of parents giving their children silly names. My views on this matter are on the record. I have stated publicly that naming a child after a store—Tiffany, for instance, or Kmart—is probably unwise. When my friend Ruthie, who was four at the time, said she wanted to name the new baby her mother was expecting Static Cling, I argued against it. Twenty years ago, I counseled that Sunshine was not a good name for a child, although perhaps perfect for a detergent. I disapproved of the slogan names favored by Chinese Communists in the fifties because, let's face it, Assist the Brave Workers of Korea is no name to have on the playground.

But if Sunshine feels more like a Norbert when he grows up—maybe he thinks Norbert is more appropriate for someone keen on regular promotions in the actuarial department—he can simply change his name. His mother, who changed her name from Maxine to Starglow when she dropped out of college in 1971 to become a mushroom gatherer, can still picture that sweetly dirty little toddler as Sunshine. Should any of this have anything to do with government clerks? Get serious.

June 10, 1991

The other day I managed to get a glimpse of the future and the past at the same time: I saw an item reporting that Barry Goldwater had gone back to being publicly pro-choice and another item reporting that the most recently transcribed tapes from Richard Nixon's Oval Office reveal him once more as a vindictive, unscrupulous paranoid. It's always comforting for a citizen to come upon confirmation that the nation's political leaders remain consistent in their character and beliefs.

Nixon was caught by his own taping system questioning his staff about the uplifting concerns we've come to identify with him: who was and who wasn't Jewish among defendants in the Chicago show trial of those who opposed the war in Vietnam, how IRS information could be acquired illegally and used against Democrats, whether some Teamsters could be induced to beat up war demonstrators. It was, in other words, what students of the Nixon presidency have come to think of as the usual Oval Office chitchat.

The release of the White House tapes gradually over the years has turned out to be a trial for poor Nixon as he tries to rehabilitate himself with ponderous pronouncements on foreign policy. He's like a mobster who, seeking respectability as he gets on in years, talks at great length to the dignitaries he has invited to tea about his legitimate business enterprises and his far-flung charities but keeps getting interrupted by flunkies who want to know where to deposit the loansharking take or how to dispose of the body of a business associate with whom there was a small disagreement.

Goldwater, whose moment in the sun was in the days before you had to hold up a placard with an aborted fetus on it in order to get the Republican nomination, apparently didn't have much to say on the subject of abortion while he was the far right's main man. Now he has publicly given his support to those Republicans who believe that the party ought to have room for people who are pro-choice—a position that the anti-abortion zealots treat as they might treat the decision of a prominent vestryman who announces that he is resigning his duties at the church in order to devote more time to his hobby of consorting with a pack of murderers.

Naturally, all this got me thinking about George Bush. I don't mean for a moment that a tape recorder under his desk might pick up the sort of ranting that took place in the Nixon White House. It was class resentment that gave Nixon's whining that exquisite timbre, and Bush, of course, has none of that, having himself been born into the class Nixon resented.

Bush is also presumably above Nixon's yahoo anti-Semitism, although he has consistently been a promoter of Fred Malek, the White House aide who was instructed by Nixon, on a previously released tape, to gather up the names of Jews who worked in the Bureau of Labor Statistics, presumably for the purpose of purging the members of the Jewish conspiracy that Nixon fantasized was responsible for some unwelcome quarterly numbers. Malek's defenders say he stalled before furnishing the names, hoping Nixon would forget—meaning that his courage in resisting a repugnant order could be celebrated on his tombstone with the phrase "He Had to Be Asked Twice."

Bush, of course, would never stoop to sending thugs in hard hats to break up antiwar demonstrations. John Sununu and C. Boyden Gray, the people he sent to break up a meeting between business and civil rights leaders that might have brought agreement on the civil rights bill and thus robbed the Administration of the quota issue to use as its Willie Horton in the 1992 campaign, are always seen in coats and ties.

And nobody in Washington thinks a gentleman like Bush is a real hater, the way the people the Willie Horton ad was meant to appeal to are haters. After he retires, I can see him putting in some time on the board of the United Negro College Fund, to which he and his father before him have contributed, and expressing some mild regret about what some aides did, without his knowledge, that might have seemed like race-baiting.

I can also see him returning to the old pro-choice position he had before he was made to understand that a pro-choice candidate couldn't be Reagan's running mate in 1980. Does anybody think it's necessary for George Bush to end his days as the only Eastern Establishment Episcopalian in the entire country who is publicly pro-life?

No, I can see Bush returning to the moderate Republicanism of his friends and relatives—unscathed and, of course, untaped. No wonder Nixon resents the upper class.

July 15, 1991

According to the *Toronto Globe and Mail,* which got its information from Reuters, "A young man in Bangkok, denied a motorcycle by his parents, locked himself in his room and has stayed there for 22 years." Talk about stubborn!

When I read about the young man in Bangkok, I turned immediately to the *Guinness Book of Records*—I wanted to see if it was possible that the official world record for longest teenage snit could be held by someone other than an American kid—but no record was listed. Even if there had been, would a forty-two-year-old man be eligible?

Reuters apparently ran across the long-term snit story in a mass-circulation Thai-language newspaper called the *Daily News,* which said that the young man who was denied the motorcycle, Dan Jaimun, permits only his younger sister to visit him in his room. At this point the younger sister must be, as my father would have put it, no spring chicken herself.

Meals are left outside the door. According to the item in the *Globe and Mail,* "The parents of Dan Jaimun tearfully asked readers of the *Daily News* to come up with ideas on how they might persuade their son to emerge from his small bedroom."

Although my wife is not a reader of the *Daily News* in Thailand—and therefore technically not one of those asked for advice by a weeping Mr. and Mrs. Jaimun—she was kind enough to offer the benefit of her experience the moment I informed her of the situation.

"Quit leaving the meals outside his door," she said. "And give him the motorcycle."

I think that's called the old carrot-and-stick approach, and it might do the trick at the Jaimun household. On questions of how to handle these family matters I have always found my wife to be very sound. A few years ago, for instance, I benefited from her observation that there must be better ways to get teenagers to quit saying "like" at the dinner table ("Like, he was like, 'Like, O.K.' ") than to threaten to place them in foster care.

Still, I told my wife I wasn't altogether certain that her plan would work in the case of Dan Jaimun. "The possibility of not leaving Dan's food outside his bedroom door must have occurred to Mr. and Mrs. Jaimun within the first five or ten years," I said. "It's possible that their son responded to the threatened end of room service by saying, 'Fine. Perfect. I'll starve to death. Life without a motorcycle isn't worth living anyway.' "

"They could try leaving meals of just carrots outside his door," said one of my daughters, who hates carrots. When she's talking about the carrot-and-stick approach, the carrot is meant literally, and it's the stick.

Around our neighborhood, there were any number of inventive ideas for getting Dan out of his room. Mr. Stone, who lives down the street, said that the Jaimuns should hire some motorcyclists to rev their motors outside the house and shout, loud enough for Dan Jaimun to hear, "Mrs. Jaimun, can Dan come out to play?" Mrs. Johnson, who lives across the street and had always struck me as a gentle sort, said, "In such situations, I have always found that one effective and humane tool a parent should consider employing is tear gas."

What surprised me about the response of my neighbors to the problem was that a number of people didn't think luring Dan from his room was necessarily the goal that Mr. and Mrs. Jaimun should concentrate on. For instance, Mr. Collins, who lives a couple of houses down, said, "Children must learn that when you say no you mean no, and for some children it takes a long time for that to sink in." Mrs. Stone, who has reared three children, said, "The important thing is to make sure he keeps that room neat and tidy. If you train a child to keep his room neat and tidy, everything else falls into place."

July 29, 1991

I went to Paris, France, and got bitten by a chigger. Was I upset? Yes, I think you could say I was a little upset.

I have spoken before about what my wife insists on calling my morbid fear of chiggers. I have spoken before about how the itch of a chigger bite is equal to approximately seven milamoses (a milamos is a unit of measurement I devised to stand for the itch power of a thousand mosquito bites). I have revealed that the itch of a chigger bite lasts just short of eternity and that the only thing that can stop it—sometimes—is amputation.

I have explained that my wife can't appreciate any of this because she's from the East and chiggers exist only in the Midwest and the South—during the summer, particularly in Kansas City, Missouri, in the tall grass next to my cousin Kenny's house.

If chiggers exist only in the Midwest and the South, you say, how did I get a chigger bite in Paris, France? That's the whole point. That's why I think you could say I was a little upset. I had thought I was safe. Am I really saying that I went to Paris to escape chiggers? Almost.

What I mean is that for someone who grew up in the Midwest, part of the pleasure of foreign travel is knowing that you're in a place where there aren't any chiggers. When someone from, say, Sedalia, Missouri, is on the top of the Eiffel Tower, looking out over the whole City of Light, what runs through his mind is, "Even if they were around here, they couldn't get this high."

You think that's weird? You think the traveler from Sedalia should be thinking about the beauty of Paris or the place of Paris in the history of Western civilization? Then you've never been bitten by a chigger.

Also, part of everyone's sense of security is the comforting notion that certain kinds of disasters only happen somewhere else. When the anchorman reports that some fabulously expensive houses perched in the Hollywood Hills have been carried off by a mudslide, people on the Great Plains breathe a sigh of relief that someone living on an absolutely flat surface is free from the threat of sliding mud.

Once, during some hard times in midwestern agriculture, I asked a wheat farmer in Nebraska if he saw any bright spots, and he said, "I figure we're pretty safe here from tidal waves." By the same token, a Hollywood producer who grew up in Hutchinson, Kansas, may wake up every morning haunted by his problems—his deal may never be made, his wife may leave with the pool boy— and cheer himself up enough to get out of bed with the thought that the day will surely pass without a tornado. We depend on these things staying where they belong.

"It can't be a chigger," my wife said. "Chiggers are only in the Midwest and the South. You told me that's why you moved to New York."

"Maybe it came over in somebody's cuff," I said. "The man sitting next to me on the plane looked suspiciously like someone I used to know from Conway, Arkansas. Or maybe they really do have chiggers in Paris, France, and the government has suppressed the information because otherwise the tourist industry would collapse. I wish I could understand French better. If the radio stations carry tornado warnings, we all have a lot more to worry about than I thought."

Then a friend of ours who lives in France informed us that what I had was an aoûtat bite—common in France, particularly in the month of August. He even showed us the definition in a French dictionary: the larva of something the French call a trombidion, which does sound itchy.

"Doesn't that make you feel better?" my wife asked.

"It would," I said, "except for this itch."

A week or so after we got home, I happened to be up very early one morning—I was up very early because of the itching—and I got curious about the word "trombidion." I couldn't find a French-English dictionary, but, just on a hunch, I looked it up in an English dictionary. I found the word "trombidiasis." It was defined as an infestation with chiggers.

So they do have chiggers in Paris, France. Probably tornados, too. I felt a lot of the premises I've operated on crumbling away. Were there also chiggers in New York, simply covered over temporarily by concrete? Should I move back to Kansas City? Or would I be at risk there from tidal waves?

CHINESE GOLF

August 19, 1991

Just as we thought things were calming down a bit inter-
nationally, a Chinese academic, Professor Ling Hong-ling,
has gone and upset the Scots by claiming that golf was
invented in China.

I know what you're thinking: this is going to remind
the Russians that they used to claim they invented baseball, which will provoke the English (who really did invent
baseball but got tired a long time ago of arguing with
people from Cooperstown) to talk about having invented
ice hockey, which will enrage the Canadians (who hardly
ever get mad) and provoke the Lithuanians into claiming
the invention of darts, and that will lead into a sort of
chain reaction of claims and counterclaims until—
powee!—World War III.

I wish I had some reassuring words about that possibility, but I have to report that—according to a piece in
the *Toronto Globe and Mail* by Carl Honoré, which is
where I read all about this—the Scots are angry as hor-
nets. Scottish tabloids have referred to Professor Hong-
ling as "a nutty, oriental professor" and an "Eastern
bogey man," the *Globe and Mail* article says, and Bobby
Burnet, golf historian to the Royal and Ancient Golf Club
in St. Andrews, is quoted as calling the whole business
"a load of malarkey."

It is only a matter of time, I think, before some Scottish golfer gets mad enough to point out that Professor Ling Hong-ling's name sounds more like a Ping-Pong match than a round of golf.

Writing in the *Australian Society for Sports History Bulletin*—a journal, I should admit, that I might have missed had the alert Honoré not pointed the way—Professor Hong-ling concluded from pottery depictions and murals and other evidence that a game very much like modern golf was played in China around the middle of the tenth century, five hundred years before the Scots claim to have invented it. It was called *chiuwan*, or hitting ball—which, you have to admit, is a much more logical name for the sport than golf, even though, during my brief fling at it many years ago, I often missed the ball completely.

Burnet tried in the *Globe and Mail* piece to explain away the pottery and murals: "If you take any kind of patterned plate or blanket or stained glass and play around with it long enough, you'll soon find a man holding a club and hitting a ball towards a hole." Being an open-minded person, I tried this theory with an old patterned plate, and it didn't work. After looking at the design for twenty minutes (some of that time squinty-eyed), what I thought I saw was a man in an undershirt eating a herring. What I'm saying is that Burnet's attempt to explain away Ling Hong-ling's murals may say less about the history of golf than it does about Burnet, or me.

As I understand Ling Hong-ling's theory, he believes some early traveler to China brought golf back to Europe, the way Marco Polo is said to have brought back to Italy what Italians came to call pasta and the way more recent travelers from the West have brought back hot tips on how a government can get rid of students who are demonstrating for democracy in large public squares.

As you might imagine, this early-traveler theory does not have a big following in Scotland, where, according to the *Globe and Mail*, "Golf sits snugly alongside clan tartan, whiskey and haggis as a symbol of Scottish ingenuity." I should say right off the bat that I have tasted haggis—it is described in my dictionary, rather discreetly, as a pudding "made of the heart, liver, and lungs of a sheep or a calf, minced with suet, onions, oatmeal, and seasonings and boiled in the stomach of the animal"— and if the Scots are worried about somebody else taking credit for inventing it, I think I can put their mind at rest on that score.

I think they're also overreacting in talking about the threat this may represent to the Scottish industry that is based on foreigners going over there to play golf on Scottish courses. Rich Americans and Japanese do not go to Scotland, wearing funny costumes and lugging golf clubs, because they believe that golf was invented by the Scots; they go there because they like the whisky.

I do believe that if the Scots will just calm down, we can ride this one out. I think it should start with Bobby Burnet apologizing for the harsh language he's used about Professor Ling Hong-ling. They should meet like gentlemen, perhaps over a round of hitting ball.

September 9, 1991

This would be a good time to stop sending me household hints on how to avoid losing one sock from a pair in the wash. I don't mean to seem unappreciative. I do value your concern. But I think this would be a good time to stop. Please.

I hope it doesn't sound ungrateful for me to say that I didn't actually ask for this advice. Some weeks ago, I'll admit, I did mention that many single socks had been lost at our house and that installing the washer-dryer right across from the bedroom rather than in the basement had no effect whatsoever on this phenomenon. This was reported, though, in the course of explaining why I didn't find it surprising that a magazine I write for lost seventy-two boxes of archives while moving from a building in midtown Manhattan to another building right across the street.

The point was not that I was searching for a way to reduce sock loss. The point was that our experience with the relocated washer-dryer, like the magazine's experience in moving the boxes, had confirmed a law of nature. The distance a pair of socks had to travel from the machine to the sock drawer, like the distance the boxes of archives had to travel, turned out not to be relevant. As in any number of other endeavors, such as airplane transportation or ski-jumping, the difficult part is at the beginning and the end, not the middle. That's a law of nature being confirmed. It just happens to be called the Law of the Single Sock.

So—and I hope I'm not sounding bossy here—if you wanted to contribute something from your own experience to the discussion, it might have been appropriate to write about some other confirmation of the Law of the Single Sock. You might have written about the time you filled a mold with brass for the bust you were making of your filthy-rich and aging and childless Uncle Hiram. Waiting for the brass to harden (the middle) was easy. It wasn't until you cracked open the mold (the end) that Uncle Hiram's left ear fell off.

Also—and I hesitate to bring this up, because I don't want to appear to be the sort of person who can't let bygones be bygones—when I actually did write a column that was obviously meant to attract some useful household hints, you people were simply not heard from. That was when my friend Jane thought a cockroach had crawled inside her computer. Jane received no help at all with her problem, and, I'm sorry to have to report, her computer is now virtually a hollow shell. Jane manages on an old Underwood office model and occasionally shoots me a glance that I interpret as meaning, "How could your people have let me down when I was calling out for help?" But never mind. I don't want to dwell on the past.

I did want to mention that the household hints you sent in about the problem of losing single socks in the laundry truly did—and I don't want to sound cranky or ungrateful here—stink.

That's right: they were simply no good. Some people thought, for instance, that I could make everything O.K. by buying only one type of socks, so that I wouldn't have a number of pairs but rather what amounted to one large gaggle of identical socks. Dandy. These are people who want me described on the tennis court as "the awkward one wearing charcoal gray above-the-calves" or maybe at a black-tie banquet as "the suave dude in the corner sporting sweat socks."

The other principal line of advice had to do with how simple and well-organized life is if every member of a typical American family safety-pins a pair of dirty socks together before depositing them in the laundry hamper and simply removes the pin before putting on a pair of clean socks. Lovely. I hear little Jenny shouting from upstairs, "Mommy, Mommy, Jason is using his sock pins to pin my ears together!" I see Dad—good old Dad, who thought moving the washer-dryer near the bedroom would solve everything—putting on his socks one morning when he happens to be distracted by having received so many household hints he didn't ask for, forgetting all about the safety pin, starting toward the closet to get his shoes, and falling on his face. Thanks.

ERRANDS

September 16, 1991

I've been back from the summer cottage for a while now, but I still seem to spend most of my time doing the sort of things that the recent biography of William Paley says he never had to do.

These biographies of the mighty stir conflicting emotions in the ordinary reader. For instance, Paley, the founder of CBS, is revealed as a liar, a braggart, a bully, a turncoat, a philanderer, and the sort of parent who in a just world would be tossed in the slammer for dereliction of duty—in other words, the sort of person we're used to reading about lately in biographies of our country's most prominent citizens. On the other hand, he never had to unpack his own car.

This combination is what stirs the conflicting emotions. If you're reading the book on the beach, you might think, "What a thoroughly loathsome human being." But if you're reading it in the license-renewal line at the Motor Vehicle Bureau—the line you're afraid you might wait in for forty minutes only to be told that the form you've filled out with such care is of no use without the birth certificate you keep in the safety deposit box—you might think, a bit wistfully, "I guess Bill Paley would have had somebody to take care of this sort of thing for him."

You would be half right. As I understand it, he would have had two people to take care of that sort of thing—

one to stand in the line at the Motor Vehicle Bureau and one who was in charge of such matters as sending somebody down to the Motor Vehicle Bureau to stand in line. This, at least, is what I was advised by my wife, who was the person in our family actually reading the book. I wanted to get to it myself, but I was too busy unpacking the car.

"When the Paleys flew from one of their houses to another, they didn't even carry a suitcase," she said. "There were people who went ahead of them to make sure that the closets were in order and the refrigerator was stocked and there were fresh flowers in the house."

Again, if I had been told that while I was lying quietly in the hammock, I might have taken it in as a marginally interesting fact about the habits of the rich. My response had to do with the fact that I was at that moment trying to balance a pile of underwear in one hand while violently pulling on a drawer that seemed to have an old American Polled Hereford Association T-shirt stuck in it in a way that prevented it from being opened more than three or four inches.

I let go of the drawer and paused, still holding the pile of underwear teetering in one hand. "I really shouldn't be doing this," I said to my wife.

"No, you shouldn't," my wife said. "If you threw out that junk you have in the lower drawer and put the underwear in there instead, you wouldn't keep getting that drawer jammed."

"I mean I shouldn't be spending my time unpacking clothes and trying to open drawers that are jammed by American Polled Hereford Association T-shirts."

"Not if you're going to get to the cleaners before they close," she said. "I finally got the washing-machine repairman to answer the phone, but I have to leave for my meeting in five minutes if I'm going to stop at the post office. You should probably run over to the cleaners now and finish unpacking later, after you change that one light bulb in the hall."

"What I meant," I said, "is that I really should have people dealing with these things for me. Didn't you tell me that until he went to check the display of some CBS magazine Paley had never been in a supermarket?"

"I don't think you'd be happy having someone else go to the supermarket," my wife said. "You couldn't trust anyone else to come across those weird brands of diet root beer you like."

But it would give me a lot more time. Of course, when Paley had a lot more time, he used it to cheat on his wife and plot against the colleagues who trusted him. Maybe he would have been better off spending a little more time going to the supermarket and standing in Motor Vehicle Bureau lines. I thought about that for a while and looked at the underwear in my hand. "Is it possible that organizing one's own underwear drawer is the path to virtue?" I asked my wife.

"Maybe you'd better take a little break," she said. "You're beginning to talk funny. We can pick up the cleaning tomorrow."

POLITE SOCIETY

Here's what I would like to say to the Rev. Ian Gregory, who has founded the Polite Society to increase the level of courtesy in England: "Buzz off, Gregory. Get lost. Take a walk. G'wan, get out of here."

I think that would get the good reverend's attention. Then I would be able to tell him, without fear of being interrupted by one of his irritating interjections—you have to guard against such people tossing in comments like "Oh, do go on" or "My, how very interesting"—that there is entirely too much courtesy in England as it is.

The author of the *New York Times* piece that brought the Rev. Gregory to my attention, William E. Schmidt, seemed quite aware that starting a Polite Society in England has a certain coals-to-Newcastle quality to it. He quotes an Italian writer named Beppe Severgnini who "reported in a recent book that Britain is the only nation he has been in where it takes four 'thank-you's' to negotiate a bus ticket."

The most irritating thank-you of the lot is the first one, which the bus conductor utters as he stands in front of the passenger, ready to collect the fare. It's obvious that the passenger has done nothing for which he should be thanked. According to Severgnini, that first thank-you actually means "I'm here." It could also mean that the conductor is giving warning that he means to out-thank-you the passenger in order to make the passenger feel like a mannerless clod.

If the passenger is an American who is intent on not being taken for one of those rude Yanks, there could be big trouble. I've warned in the past about the dangers inherent in an American trying to out-thank-you an English person. The exchange of thank-you's goes on and on, and the American may see no way to end it except to take out a semi-automatic rifle and shoot the English person.

I suspect the Rev. Ian Gregory would take exception to this approach, to which I would reply, "Mind your own business, Gregory." Once that put him in a frame of mind to listen, I would remind him that he lives in a country where a man who did carry coal to Newcastle would, upon arriving at the place where the coal was supposed to be delivered, hand over the bill of lading and say "Thank you."

Get this picture: A large delivery of coal has just been made to someone in Newcastle who is up to his armpits in coal. The air is heavy with coal dust. Every time the person receiving the delivery wipes his brow—which he does pretty often, since he has broken out in a cold sweat trying to imagine what he's going to do with more coal—he leaves a thick black smudge on his head. And the ding-dong who has made the delivery is standing there saying "Thank you." It makes you wonder why there isn't more violence in England. I suppose it's a good thing that people there aren't allowed to have semi-automatic rifles.

To be fair to the Rev. Ian Gregory—and I don't know why I should be; call me an old softie—he does distinguish between what he calls "genuinely considerate behavior" and simply littering your conversation with a lot of extraneous thank-you's. What makes the work of the Polite Society necessary, he told Schmidt, is the sort of backsliding in considerate behavior that Margaret Thatcher was referring to when she said, "Graciousness is being replaced by surliness in much of everyday life."

What I would say to that is, "In a pig's eye, Gregory." Having thus given him ample notice that I might have a differing view, I would remind him that Margaret Thatcher and genuinely considerate behavior were strangers. She was known throughout the realm, for instance, for bullying and humiliating her own cabinet ministers. What she meant by graciousness was being respectful to people like her.

To which I think the proper response would be "Stick it in your ear, Mac." Which is simply a way of saying that I think genuinely considerate behavior is the sort of thing that might be practiced by an American on a London bus who realizes that answering the conductor's thank-you with another thank-you could start a spiral into violence. Armed with that knowledge, he could actually be doing the bus conductor a favor in the long run if he answered that first absurd thank-you by saying, "Watch your mouth, buddy," or "Listen, Mac, you looking to get your face rearranged?"

The problem is the response he would almost certainly get from the bus conductor: "Thank you."

October 14, 1991

I guess the Scandinavians who arranged to have replicas of Leif Ericsson's boats sail from Norway to North America this year didn't realize what trouble Columbus is in.

I can understand that the situation must have looked entirely different when they began putting the trip together a few years ago. They must have figured that with everybody in both North and South America planning to make a big deal in 1992 out of the five-hundredth anniversary of Christopher Columbus's voyages, they would take the wind out of Columbus's sails—apparently something God used to do with some regularity in 1492—by sailing here in Viking boats just before that to remind everyone which European explorer got to the Western Hemisphere hundreds of years before Columbus was born.

The reason I assume their motive was to steal Columbus's thunder—something God never did in 1492 because He knew that thunder could scare fifteenth-century sailors right out of their skivvies—is that this sounds very much like part of an argument that has been going on in this country as long as anybody can remember. The argument is over who got here first.

For years, Italian-Americans have been dismissing Leif Ericsson as some pirate with horns on his hat, and Scandinavian-Americans have been referring to Colum-

bus as "that Italian guy who got lost a few years ago."
Meanwhile, Irish-Americans say that both Ericsson and
Columbus were centuries behind a monk named Brendan the Navigator, who popped over from Ireland in the
middle of the sixth century.

All of this is perfectly understandable, of course, in
a country made up of immigrant groups who arrive with
a tenuous hold on their position in an adopted land and
find that a lot of people already here are prone to shout,
"Go back where you came from."

It wouldn't surprise me to hear that some Greek-
Americans have persuasive evidence that when Brendan
and his party landed on the shores of Cape Cod he found
that a model of the Parthenon had been built in the sand.
It wouldn't surprise me to hear that one of the Jewish-
American scholars who now have access to the Dead Sea
Scrolls for the first time will claim to have found a passage that could be interpreted to mean that a world across
the sea was discovered in the second century by an explorer named Moishe the Lionhearted. When the recent
immigrants from Southeast Asia get a generation or two
as Americans under their belt, it would be perfectly natural for them to come up with an ancient Asian map of
North America and remind everyone that they are not
called boat people for nothing.

Or it would have been perfectly natural at one time.
Now, as the five-hundredth anniversary of Columbus's
voyage approaches, some Americans are making it clear
that they don't consider getting here first from the other
side of the Atlantic (or the Pacific) anything to brag
about. They say that these explorers didn't "discover" a
New World, because a lot of people were already here,
living in ancient and complex societies that, unlike the
European society of that era, encouraged regular bathing.
They say that what the explorers brought was disease and

slavery and a whole lot more sludge than you'd feel comfortable talking about.

Without getting into the question of who's right about whether Columbus's voyages should be called voyages of discovery and whether they should be considered cause for celebration—there are some places you tread only at the risk of having a lot of people shout at you, "Go back where you came from"—I have to point out that this new argument has to affect the old argument about who got here first. If the first European on these shores brought practically nothing but trouble, who wants to claim him?

So I can see some Irish-American zealots reconsidering any campaign they might have been planning to force the capital of the Buckeye State to change its name to Brendan, Ohio. I can envision a speaker at an Ancient Order of the Hibernians meeting being cheered as, refuting charges that Brendan was responsible for turning this continent into a sinkhole, he quotes Samuel Eliot Morrison, the great historian of American settlement, to prove that the place referred to in Brendan's journal was probably the Azores rather than Massachusetts.

At the same time, a lot of people of Norwegian and Swedish and Danish descent are trying to persuade the city officials of Minneapolis that holding a large parade in October every year is the least they can do to honor the discoverer of America, Christopher Columbus. Meanwhile, the replicas of Leif Ericsson's ships quietly slip out to sea, hoping they'll be mistaken for Russian trawlers.

I'M O.K., I'M NOT O.K.

November 4, 1991

First I heard on the radio about a new "happy-to-be-me" doll, which is thicker at the waist and hips than the idealized doll that we've been accustomed to and also has bigger feet. Then I came across a story I had clipped out of the *New York Times* a couple of months back about how plastic surgeons can now fill out the wrinkles on a patient's face with fat taken from somewhere else on his body—a procedure that a Beverly Hills plastic surgeon called "the epitome of recycling." Sometimes, I have to admit, I wonder about this country.

What I'm wondering this time is how in a single society so many people can make money on the proposition that you are truly fine just as you are (the self-esteem industry) while so many other people are making money on the proposition that there are no limits to the ways you can improve the wreck you find yourself to be (the self-improvement industry).

Every year, two or three different pop psychologists haul in a bundle with self-help books whose titles amount to some version of *You Are the Very Best Person in the Whole Wide World*. Of course, it's perfectly possible that a person who buys one of these books is not, in fact, the very best person in the whole wide world; the cashier at the bookstore doesn't do any testing. It's perfectly possible, in fact, that a person who buys one of these books is a crumb-bum. Or maybe he's just a perfectly O.K. person who's a little thick in the waist and has big feet.

But the book is so convincing that the person who buys it—let's call him Harvey—sails along for months, absolutely stinky with self-esteem. He has even begun to feel a little sorry for people who have normal-sized feet and are therefore much more vulnerable to being toppled in a high wind.

At the same time, though, he is constantly being bombarded with suggestions that he is not only not the best person in the whole wide world but a walking disaster area. Every time he turns on the television he is reminded that he is overweight and afflicted with a flaking scalp and occasionally irregular and ignorant of the most rudimentary notions of personal investment strategy. When he goes to the bookstore to browse for new books telling him how terrific he is, he notices books with titles like *Get That Waistline Down* and *How to Take Inches Off Those Feet.* And his morale isn't helped by the fact that anytime columnists want to indicate that someone might have low self-esteem they name him Harvey.

So Harvey is on kind of a roller coaster. One day he's on top of the world, even though he's having a little trouble getting his pants buttoned over that waist of his, and the next day he feels the self-esteem drain out of him like crankcase oil that needed changing a long time ago.

When he feels like that, he goes back down to the bookstore and finds something with a title like *There's Absolutely Nobody Better Than You* and gets a little booster shot of self-confidence.

From reading these books Harvey has learned just how to handle anything that threatens to undermine his belief that there is nobody in the world better than he is. He is quite aware of the possibility that at any time someone might say to him, "Have you ever noticed that you're a little thicker in the waist than a lot of people?" or even "You know, you've got a wrinkle or two near the mouth there that could be filled out by fat taken from some part of your body where, not to put too fine a point on this, you wouldn't really miss it."

If that happens, Harvey knows to say, "I've been given reason to believe that I'm the very best person in the whole wide world, although I don't like to boast."

If the same person goes on to say, "Are those your feet or is there a ski slope around here I didn't notice?" Harvey knows to say, "I'm happy to be me."

There may be a time, though, when a confrontation like that shakes Harvey's confidence. So he goes over to the mall to look for another book with a title like *You're It, Big Guy*. But the bookstore is closed. For a moment Harvey is crushed. Then he notices that the toystore next door is still open. He rushes in and says, "Do you have a happy-to-be-me doll?" They do. Harvey is O.K. again.

December 2, 1991
I wasn't surprised by the discovery that the question-and-answer sessions President Bush has when he addresses conventions and banquets via closed-circuit television are scripted in advance. That sort of thing goes on around here all the time.

For instance, some old friends of ours, Hank and Betsy Garland, sometimes give me a list of questions to ask their nineteen-year-old son, Nick. They say it's the only way they can get any information out of him. I'm told this is a very common condition among nineteen-year-old boys.

Apparently, when the Garlands phone Nick at college, it's like talking to someone who's seen too many movies about how prisoners of war are supposed to say nothing beyond their name, rank, and serial number.

At the dinner table Betsy Garland might say something to Nick like, "So apparently the Miller boy has decided to go to law school because he figures a law degree will never hurt you, whether you actually practice or not, and he thinks it's the sort of thing you're better off doing right away because if not, who knows when you'll ever feel like going back to school even if you think it's basically something that will stand you in good stead, which makes a lot of sense to me, doesn't it to you?"

And Nick will say, if he's in a particularly loquacious mood, "I guess."

The Garlands have reason to believe that when Nick is talking to people who are not related to him he carries on normal conversations. So whenever we all get together while Nick is home for the holidays, Betsy and Hank Garland phone ahead to go over a list of questions they'd like me to ask Nick, preferably when one of them is standing nearby.

The first time the Garlands asked if they could plant some questions with me, I was reluctant. It sounded a little sneaky, and Nick and I, after all, go way back. But Betsy Garland assured me there was nothing at all wrong with it. "We just want to make sure certain topics are covered," she said.

That's pretty much what the White House said, after a microphone that the president didn't know was open recorded him complaining that the folks attending the Association of Christian Schools International convention in Anaheim, California, hadn't asked their spontaneous questions in the assigned order.

If the White House didn't plant the questions, somebody who had just lost his job might ask the president about why the economy is so rotten instead of asking about why the liberals are so intent on imposing quotas on the American people and (next question, Mr. President: please turn the page) coddling vicious criminals.

One difference between the White House and our crowd, in addition to the fact that we make do without closed-circuit television, is that we script only the question half of the exchange. I have no idea what Nick is going to answer, and his parents, of course, know a lot less than I do. In that way, it's more like the Reagan White House—full of surprises.

For instance, when we were at the Garlands' recently, I was under instructions to find out whether Nick has a serious girlfriend. I was encouraged to put the question any way I wanted to—"Well, Nick, could it be said that there's a sweetie-pie in the picture?" or "Tell me: are wedding bells breaking up that old gang of mine?"

As Nick and I chatted near the buffet table, the Garlands drifted closer; Hank, as a cover, poured Betsy some more cider. I asked the question in a rather roundabout way, and as Nick answered, I noticed that his father had become so engrossed that he kept pouring the cider long after Betsy's glass was full.

Just as Betsy became aware of a stream of cider on her foot, Nick said it would be hard to tell how serious this relationship was until he and the young woman in question traveled in Europe for a while that summer, and Hank—shouting, "What Europe? Who said anything about Europe?"—dropped the cider bottle into the turkey gravy.

Both Hank and Betsy seemed quite upset as the three of us worked to clean up the mess. "Don't worry about it," I said, trying to make them feel better. "This sort of thing happens at the White House all the time."

January 27, 1992

Once my wife had informed me that a parking ticket in Tokyo could cost $1,400, I felt a lot better.

I had just gotten a parking ticket in New York, under circumstances that I found, well, dispiriting, and my wife was trying to cheer me up. "The most expensive ticket in New York is two hundred dollars," she said. "That's only one seventh what it is in Tokyo. And your ticket is for fifty dollars, which is only a quarter of the maximum fine." My wife was very good at fractions when she was in school, and that has permitted her to see the bright side ever since.

Seeing the bright side usually involves knowing about a dark side somewhere else, whether fractions are involved or not. The cost of a parking ticket in Tokyo is typical of the facts she has in what I think of as her count-your-blessings file.

Recently, for instance, I found that somebody had taken a whack at the driver's door of my car with a blunt instrument, for no reason I could imagine. When I told that to my wife, she reminded me that we had read about a contretemps in Kansas City in which the proprietor of a store dealing in kosher specialties flung a jar of gefilte fish through the windshield of a customer's car.

"That could never happen here," my wife said.

She was right. We're pretty much safe from having

tradesmen fling jars of gefilte fish in our direction. In the first place, people in New York ordinarily do their shopping on foot rather than in cars. Also, no store dealing in kosher specialties in New York would think of selling gefilte fish in a jar rather than fresh.

I was so grateful for the improvement in my mood that I thanked my wife once again for the help she had given me several weeks before, when I injured my thumb attempting to hang a picture in our living room. My wife had immediately brought to my attention the woman in Key West we read about last fall in an Associated Press item as follows: "KEY WEST, FLA. (AP)—A drowsy asthma sufferer who grabbed the gun under her pillow rather than the inhaler she keeps there was hospitalized with a bullet wound to the face."

According to the Associated Press, the asthma sufferer, an aircraft maintenance worker at the Boca Chica Naval Air Station, was in what she called "kind of transition" between sleep and consciousness when she plugged herself in the jaw under the impression that she was taking a belt from her inhaler. The shot went through the pillow, and she wasn't hurt badly.

"It's true that I have never shot myself in the face in my sleep," I said.

Actually, I don't own a gun. The Second Amendment to the Constitution reads, "A well regulated Militia being necessary to the security of a free State, the right of the people to keep and bear Arms shall not be infringed." The way I read that, if I keep and bear arms somebody might get the idea that I'd be a good person to draft into a well-regulated militia. So I decided not to take any chances, even before I realized that a person with a gun under his pillow could very easily shoot himself in the face by mistake.

"You don't even have asthma," my wife said.

Also true. Actually, I sleep pretty well, except on Saturday nights. We live in Greenwich Village, which, as I have mentioned before, is where a lot of people from the suburbs go on Saturday nights to test their car alarms.

On the Saturday after I got the door of my car fixed, one of the visitors to our neighborhood apparently became irritated; maybe he returned to his car at the end of the evening to find that his car alarm hadn't gone off once, even though several people had obviously walked within ten yards of it. In that state of mind, he ran into my car, which happened to be parked on the street— caving in both of the doors on the driver's side with such force that one of the back wheels was knocked up onto the curb.

Somebody got the license plate of the New Jersey driver, but of course the police in New York have better things to do than work out extradition arrangements with New Jersey for people who hit empty cars. The police were not completely inactive. They gave me a ticket for parking a car partly on the sidewalk.

That's the ticket I found, well, dispiriting. But then my wife told me that in Tokyo a ticket could cost $1,400. I felt a lot better.

TOO OLD

February 10, 1992

According to the *New York Times*, there is now at least
one Manhattan bar in which a customer who wants to
spice up his evening can slip into a jumpsuit with Velcro
strips on the back, race down a carpeted runway, do a
flip off a small trampoline, and see how high he ends up
stuck onto a Velcro wall upside down. This is no joke. At
least, I'm not joking; I couldn't vouch for the level of
seriousness of the people sticking upside down on the
wall.

As it happens, I'm too old for Velcro wall-jumping.
That's O.K. What strikes me immediately about this
sport, if that's what you'd call it, is that it's a good thing
to be too old for. If you weren't too old for it, you'd have
to think of another excuse.

A while back there was a brief fashion for pop psychology that concentrated on six or eight or ten phases
of life that everyone was supposed to go through. At the
time, I figured that the stages of life could be reduced to
two: the stage during which you're too young to do what
you really want to do and the stage during which you're
too old to do what you really want to do.

I knew that there could be considerable frustration
involved in being too young or too old for even things
you didn't particularly want to do. I remember when,
some years ago, I realized that I was too old to become

a Transit Authority patrolman, and found that a blow to my spirits.

For a long time I had routinely glanced at the Transit Authority Police Department's recruiting advertisements in the subway. If you were eighteen to twenty-nine and had a high school diploma and were in good general health, the ads said, you could apply for a position as a Transit Authority patrolman. One day—not a birthday; this was something that sort of snuck up on me—I was riding home on the subway when I realized that I was too old to apply.

As it happens, I had never had any desire to become a Transit Authority patrolman. Without having given the matter much thought, I knew I'd find it a trial walking around with all that stuff hanging off my belt.

Still, as I told my wife when I got home, even if you don't happen to want to go the party, it's nice to be invited.

"Don't worry about it," my wife said. "In a couple of years you're going to be old enough to be president."

As it happens, I didn't want to be president any more than I wanted to be a Transit Authority patrolman. I've admitted before that I once had a brief yearning for the presidency after I read that the president can see any movie he wants to see right in the basement of the White House, but the yearning evaporated when I read about how hard the president was working on the budget he had to submit to Congress. Any job that considers a budget a top priority, I figured, is not a job for me.

These days, of course, VCRs have made it possible for just about anyone to see any movie he wants to see right in his own living room. That may well be why Mario Cuomo decided not to run: he's known as a real homebody, and these days the movies at his home are plenty good enough. He doesn't need the White House.

But what my wife said that time about the presidency sort of disturbed me. The other way of looking at the situation she had described was this: I was in that awkward period that you go through when you're too old to become a Transit Authority patrolman and too young to be president—a sort of early-thirties no-man's-land.

That period can be pretty rough on a person. Maybe that's why a lot of people in their early thirties do weird things—of which trying to stick to Velcro walls upside down is just one I might mention.

My relief at not being upside down on a Velcro wall myself made me realize that I've passed into a third stage of life, one that I wasn't aware of when I divided life neatly in two: I'm in the stage where you find a lot of things you're grateful for being too old to do.

There's a lot to be said for this stage. I've started to make a list, and I'm enjoying it. Transit Authority patrolman is already on the list. I think it will give me great pleasure someday to add the presidency.

SPEAK SOFTLY

February 17, 1992

I was not among those who decided that President Bush's State of the Union speech failed to live up to its billing as the "defining moment" of his presidency. What could define the Bush Administration better than a speech that nobody could remember anything about two weeks later?

I had previously refused, on similar grounds, to join the general ridicule of the president's trip to Japan—the one that had originally been scheduled as an inspection tour of the New World Order and was transformed under domestic political pressure to a search for "jobs, jobs, jobs"—as a boondoggle that had no real connection with the problems of American industry. The White House's transformation of the tour was, I pointed out, a perfect statement of what ails American industry: instead of retooling, they simply repackaged.

When it comes to what might be called the president's mega-communications with the American people, in other words, you might say that I have been one of his most consistent defenders.

Now some of my brethren in the press are saying that one of the president's problems is that he doesn't have any speechwriters who can turn out memorable phrases. Again I have to advise the president to ignore this sort of criticism. When a man has nothing to say, the worst thing he can do is to say it memorably.

Remember when Dan Quayle, apparently unable to think of an appropriate platitude for the occasion, tried to borrow the motto of the United Negro College Fund ("A mind is a terrible thing to waste") and said, "What a waste it is to lose one's mind, or not to have a mind as being very wasteful. How true that is." He would have been a lot better off just mumbling something about how happy he was to be there.

Apparently, the people in the White House who don't understand these things panicked just before the State of the Union speech and brought in Peggy Noonan, who was declared the genius of Washington speech-writers during the 1988 campaign for writing—or, to be absolutely specific, picking up—the phrase "Read my lips" as a way for George Bush to promise that he would absolutely never raise taxes.

Washington speechwriters become famous these days for utilizing catchlines that have been lying around in the public vocabulary, like dandruff. The second most famous line that emerged from the presidential campaigns of the eighties—"Where's the beef?"—was lifted from a television commercial. Reagan got both of his best-known lines—"Make my day" and "Win one for the Gipper"—from movies.

Fortunately for Bush, Noonan couldn't think of any memorable phrases for the State of the Union speech. Maybe she hasn't been getting to any movies lately. The White House operatives should consider themselves lucky that Noonan hadn't just seen Gone with the Wind on videotape. The president, who has lately been trying to show his sympathy for the common man in these hard times, might have found himself saying, "Frankly, my dear, I don't give a damn."

The real problem with "Read my lips" was not that it was a stale catchline. The real problem was that as delivered by Bush in that bizarre tough-guy imitation he does, as if he were Fred Astaire playing Emiliano Zapata, it became the best-known line of the campaign.

As someone who has been in any number of political campaigns, Bush should know that all politicians make promises that they may or may not be able to keep once they get into office and that the last thing a candidate wants to do is tattoo the promise on the public memory with a particularly memorable phrase.

Memorable phrases are fine for abstract principles that are not subject to change in the face of political tactics or the quarterly GNP figures ("Ask not what your country can do for you, ask what you can do for your country"). Bush should have learned that lesson in Iowa in 1980 when, in the only memorable phrase he uttered, he charged that Reagan was talking "voodoo economics" and then found himself defending those economics in return for a spot on the ticket.

Now a dozen years of voodoo economics have helped put us all in the soup, but is there a memorable phrase that links our problems with Ronald Reagan? Of course not. That old body didn't spend all those years on the Warner Brothers lot without learning to avoid uttering the punchline of a joke that could turn sour. It's George Bush who is associated with the economics of voodoo and broken promises. Best be quiet now.

March 2, 1992
In Orlando, my cousin John and I had dinner at a place that features a medieval jousting tournament. Then we stopped to take in some bungee-jumping. I was in town only for the evening, and John wanted to make sure I saw the bright lights.

I was pretty impressed. I live in New York, where there's no restaurant at all that puts on a medieval jousting tournament. In Manhattan, the real estate alone for a place large enough for a jousting tournament would cost considerably more than the Middle Ages did. In defense of the entertainment opportunities in Manhattan, I should say that there are a number of restaurants where you can usually count on seeing some rough stuff before the evening's over.

New York doesn't have any bungee-jumping either, although every now and then someone displeased with the way the market went that day will jump off a tall building without bothering to attach himself to a cord of any kind.

When John informed me, on the way to dinner, that there were half a dozen knights in the jousting tournament, I got pretty excited. "I don't suppose you'd be interested in any side bets, would you, John?" I said.

John shook his head disapprovingly. John is a lawyer, and I figured maybe Florida has a strict law against betting on knights of the round table. I guess I've lived in New York too long. New York is a side-bet sort of place. If someone stands on top of a tall building thinking about jumping without being attached to a cord of any kind, there are a lot of side bets down below.

John explained to me that side bets really wouldn't be appropriate because the jousting is more like a show than a real contest. That close to Disney World, he said, everything is a show. I got the impression that if you were mugged in Orlando, the mugger would take off his mask afterward and give you back your money and just collect a couple of coupons from you, unless it's part of a single-admission Urban World attraction.

The jousting place was, of course, in a castle, along a double-lane lined with restaurants and motels and T-shirt shops and signs informing you that if you don't happen to like medieval jousting with your dinner you can eat in a place that has an Arabian Nights horse show instead.

In the castle eating hall, which was more like an arena than a dining room, tables were arranged in rows, like bleachers, on two sides of the large field where the horsemen perform. Our waiter—who, like everybody else on the staff, wore a costume from a Robin Hood movie—said we wouldn't have any silverware because they didn't use that sort of thing in the twelfth century. He called us "my lords" and "my ladies." We called him Duane.

Each of the knights was decked out in a different color, matching the colors on his horse. Our section was backing the blue knight, who looked just a tad wimpy to me. We were encouraged to cheer him on and boo his enemies, particularly the green knight. I got into the spirit of the thing right away. I booed the green knight and called him some awful names until a man next to me reminded me that there were children present. I guess

I've lived in New York too long. New York is an awful-name sort of place.

When the blue knight rode in front of us, I cheered and threw some infield chatter his way. ("Come boy, come baby. You the man, man. You the boy, boy. No hitter up there. You the best, you the boy, you the baby.") Then I sang the University of Missouri fight song. That made a lot of people frown at me, although one man in the yellow section stood up and yelled, "Go, you Tigers."

Our knight got killed by the green knight. "Don't worry, it's just a show," John said.

"If it's just a show," I said, "I think they could improve it by having the blue knight, just when the green knight is standing over him, about to run him through, pull an AK-47 out of his cape and put about sixty rounds in the green knight."

I was still thinking about ways to improve the show when we got to the bungee-jumping, which consisted of people being taken in the cherry-picker of a crane 150 feet above a drainage pond and then jumping out.

"Is this a show?" I asked John.

"No, these are real people," John said. "They pay fifty-five dollars for a jump."

"Great," I said. "How about some side bets?"

April 6, 1992

My friend Jean-Michel, who arrived from Paris for a visit recently, asked if I could provide him with an update on what's going on in America these days. "Absolutely no problem, J-M," I said. "Or, as you folks over there would say, *Absolument pas de problème*." As it happens, I speak a little French myself, except, of course, for verbs.

In fact, knowing that in French *pas* means "not," more or less, permits me to be a lot more sophisticated than those Wayne's World guys when it comes to what I believe linguists call the dawdling snapper. When Jean-Michel walked in, even before he could ask me what's going on in the United States, I said, "Say, Jean-Michel, that's an awfully cool necktie you're wearing today . . . *pas*."

That sort of puzzled Jean-Michel. So I told him that maybe the Wayne's World way of talking was difficult for a foreigner to understand. Then I assured him that his English is, of course, absolutely perfect. Then, after a couple of beats, I said, ". . . *pas*." Then I started giggling a lot, and Jean-Michel gave me a very stern look.

When I had pulled myself together, I told Jean-Michel that what American political candidates talk about a lot these days—aside from whether or not their opponent is guilty of having thrown spitballs in fourth grade—is how the middle class is faring. All politicians say they want to improve the lot of the middle class, I told him, which is not bad politics considering the fact that in the United States ninety percent of the population identifies itself as middle class.

"Ah, the bourgeoisie," Jean-Michel said.

"Well, not exactly," I said.

"But of course," Jean-Michel said. "Look it up."

I hate it when Jean-Michel says to look something up, because he's almost always right. He really does speak perfect English, even though he sounds a lot like Inspector Clouseau. I took out the dictionary—the English dictionary—and looked up "bourgeoisie." It said that "bourgeoisie" means the middle class.

Once I got used to the idea, I realized that public discourse on this subject could be freshened up a bit if the politicians began referring to the middle class as the bourgeoisie. It's in the dictionary that way, after all.

Think of presidential candidates insisting in their campaign debates that something has to be done to ease the economic pressures now facing the bourgeoisie. Think of a congressional leader leaning into the television camera and saying earnestly, "We have been trying to put together some package that will offer a bourgeois tax cut."

Jean-Michel happened to arrive toward the end of the New York primary campaign, so of course he was curious about the candidates, Bill Clinton and Jerry Brown. "Are they both representatives of the bourgeoisie?" he said.

"Well, not exactly," I said. "Clinton is the kid in school from a less than perfect family who will do anything to avoid a blemish on his record ('I may have thrown one spitball, but what I was really doing was carrying on an experiment having to do with wind currents, an experiment that can be seen as a reflection of my healthy curiosity and my interest in the wonders of the nature around me, and also I didn't really enjoy it very much'), and Brown is the kid who's shameless because he knows his father can put in the fix ('Sure I threw spitballs, but that was the old me')."

"Just as I thought," Jean-Michel said. "They are both representatives of the bourgeoisie. And how has the president been doing as a campaigner?"

I told Jean-Michel that on the campaign trail the president tends to jerk his arms around a lot and speak in little bursts of sentence fragments that sound as if they might be part of some other conversation carried on by two other people somewhere else on a different subject. "I think if he were campaigning in France, he wouldn't have any trouble at all winning the affection of the voters," I said, "because he's very reminiscent of Jerry Lewis."

"Ah, Jerry . . ." Jean-Michel said, smiling just at the thought. The French, of course, revere Jerry Lewis, although there is no indication that they would actually want somebody like that as their president.

"That's right, J-M," I said. "When I saw clips of Bush campaigning in New Hampshire, I half expected him to end with a pitch for funds to fight the scourge of muscular dystrophy."

"So how do the American people feel about this campaign, then?" Jean-Michel said.

"Well, we think everything's going to be just dandy," I said, ". . . *pas.*"

April 13, 1992

Every new baseball season brings renewed pressure for me to become a Kansas City fan. I'm used to it by now. When the president throws out the first ball, I know that I'll be getting a telephone call the morning after the Royals have posted their first victory. "Hey, how about those Royals!" a baseball fan I know named Gerald will say.

"How about them?" I will say, in a tone of voice that is pretty much the tone of voice I might use if someone said to me, "Hey, how about those new regulations in Title XII of the Farm Price Support Act revisions?"

When the Athletics were in Kansas City, Gerald used to say, "Hey, how about those Athletics!"

"How about them?" I always said, as if he had drawn my attention to some new statistics on urban mass transit in the European Community.

Gerald always responded to that in the same way. "I mean, you being from Kansas City and all," he'd say.

"I am from Kansas City," I would say. "But the Athletics are not. They are a Philadelphia team."

Every year I have to explain to Gerald once again that when I was a lad I rooted for the Kansas City Blues of the old American Association, the true Kansas City team. I have to explain to him that your team when you were twelve is your team forever, unless you're a Communist or something.

"The Athletics moved to Kansas City from Philadelphia," I will remind him again this year when the subject of the Royals comes up. That will cause him to say that he is talking about the Royals, not the Athletics. That will cause me to say that, as a matter of principle, I have always refused to distinguish between them. That will cause him to say that the Royals actually originated in Kansas City. That will cause me to say, "Not when I was twelve they didn't."

"The Athletics are a Philadelphia team," I will repeat. "They were led by Connie Mack. He was the oldest man in the world when I was twelve. He must be positively ancient by now."

"Connie Mack died years ago," Gerald will say.

"I'm sorry to hear it," I will say. "A real gentleman, Mr. Mack." I remind Gerald that six years ago I acknowledged publicly that my devotion to the Kansas City Blues was of such purity that their demise ended my interest in organized baseball. I no longer know which baseball managers are dead and which are alive. I feel the same way about owners. If the Red Sox are not still owned by Tom Yawkey, I don't want to know about it.

Gerald has lived in New York for forty years, but he grew up in Baltimore. He is a loyal fan of the Baltimore Orioles. In the past I have felt obligated to remind him that the Orioles arrived in Baltimore after he left town, and that he is therefore cheering for someone else's team. The Baltimore franchise was moved from St. Louis. The Orioles are actually the old St. Louis Browns, and, from what I'm told, it sometimes shows in the late innings.

"That's ridiculous," Gerald said to me. "There's no law that a person has to root for the team he rooted for when he was twelve. You live in New York now. You could root for the Yankees if you wanted to."

"I would never root for the Yankees, even if I were

still interested in organized baseball," I told Gerald. "The Blues were a Yankee farm club, and the Yankees were always calling up our best players just when we got into the stretch of a pennant race. I hate the Yankees. Any Blues fan worth his salt hates the Yankees."

"I don't know what you mean by 'any Blues fan,' " Gerald said. "The Blues haven't played for at least thirty-five years. You're the only Blues fan there is."

"I consider that a great honor," I said. "And a responsibility."

This year, Gerald wanted me to go to Baltimore with him to see a game in the new stadium. "It's a fantastic place," he said. "You can get hot dogs but you can also get crabcakes."

"I can't imagine why a St. Louis team would serve crabcakes," I told Gerald. "There aren't any crabs in the Mississippi. Actually, the specialty of St. Louis is toasted ravioli. At the least they might serve catfish. Not crabcakes."

"Why don't you drop all this silliness and come with me to an Orioles game," Gerald said.

"Maybe one of these days," I said. "Let me know the next time they have a three-game series with the Blues."

DON'T MENTION IT

May 11, 1992

Here's how this country took care of the herpes epidemic: we quit talking about it. Something worse had come along—AIDS. We talked about that so much that we more or less forgot about herpes. So it disappeared. I think that's what they must mean by the phrase "modern medical miracle."

Some years ago I saw mononucleosis taken care of the same way. When I was in college, mononucleosis was the diagnosis of choice for practically any set of symptoms. You could hardly step onto a campus without being diagnosed as having mono.

College students today never heard of mononucleosis. Did somebody discover a vaccine? Did mono change its name? I don't think so. I think it just disappeared because we quit talking about it. Remember when you got a nasty little bump and your mother said if you just quit talking about it for a while it would go away? That's how we took care of mononucleosis.

You say you know someone who has herpes? Oh, well, sure. That's perfectly possible. When I say we took care of it, I don't mean we cured it. Herpes still exists. But I hope your friend doesn't expect any sympathy, because we don't talk about it anymore. It's all over. We took care of it.

We've done that with any number of problems. Remember when vicious pit bulls were a big problem in this country? That was a scary time. When you walked down some ostensibly peaceful street in a nice residential neighborhood, you were always imagining a low growl off in the bushes.

But then we took care of vicious pit bulls the same way we took care of herpes. We quit talking about them. That was that for vicious pit bulls. I guess we showed them. You say you know someone who got bit by a vicious pit bull just a few days ago? Well, sure. It happens. But let's not make a big deal out of it. It's over.

President Reagan was a master at taking care of problems by not talking about them. Remember when the chaos in Lebanon was such a big problem that he sent the marines in to keep the peace? Then a couple of hundred marines got killed in that barracks bombing and we pulled out and Reagan simply quit talking about Lebanon? "What barracks bombing?" you say. "Which marines? Which Lebanon?" See what I mean? He took care of that one.

George Bush tried to do the same thing with the problem of racism and the conditions existing in the inner cities. You may have wondered why the Reagan-Bush people didn't establish a policy of its own if, as Marlin Fitzwater claimed, the Great Society programs they found when they came to power were just the sort of things that cause riots ("If the government puts one more Head Start program in this neighborhood, I'm going to trash the supermarket"). The answer is that they did put in a policy of their own: the policy was to not talk about it.

It wasn't exactly what Daniel Patrick Moynihan once called "benign neglect." It was more like malicious neglect, because occasionally the president would remind white voters whose side he was on—say, by insisting, long after even business leaders were satisfied with last year's civil rights bill, that he wouldn't sign it because it was a "quota bill" that would result in "reverse discrimination."

In fact, I suspect that if you did a computer search on what George Bush has said on the issue of race in America during his term of office, you'd find that he has talked more about the evil of quotas than about any other subject. In other words, despite what places like south-central Los Angeles were like even before the riots, the most consistent message the president of the United States has delivered on the question of race in the past three years is that we're in danger of giving black people too many breaks.

But that wasn't his policy. His policy was to not talk about it. The only one of Bush's cabinet secretaries who ever mentioned the problems of the inner city was Jack Kemp, and the Bush White House treated him pretty much like mononucleosis. According to documents leaked to the *New York Times*, one of the arguments used by White House aides for rejecting Kemp's notion that Bush should lead an antipoverty effort was that it could give poverty "greater visibility."

Now that the riots in Los Angeles have made all of this a leading subject of discussion, the president saves a place for Kemp on *Air Force One* and invites him around for photo opportunities and talks about how dandy his ideas are. Bush is discovering that your mother wasn't always right. Sometimes, if you don't talk about it, it won't go away after all.

June 1, 1992
When I read that the young Ross Perot's stated reason for wanting a hardship discharge before he had fulfilled his naval obligation was that sailors were always "taking God's name in vain" and behaving promiscuously on shore leave, I had to wonder whether he knew a lot less about the Navy when he was in high school than I did.

While I was growing up—in Kansas City, Missouri, just a couple of states and a few years from Perot—we were aware that sailors did not always behave absolutely respectably, particularly in foreign ports. That was part of the draw. In fact, if I had been asked to explain the traditional appeal of the Navy for the sons of the Midwest in two words, I believe those two words would have been "shore leave." We were desperately envious of shore leave. We didn't even have any shore.

We also liked the idea of all that cussing. These days, of course, it's common to hear grannies talk dirty. But when Ross and I were growing up, talking dirty in front of grownups was certainly frowned on—or maybe swatted at would be a better way to put it—and talking dirty in front of girls wasn't done much either. The Navy, we thought, offered a young man from the Midwest the opportunity to cuss all he wanted.

Lest you think the notion of sailors regularly taking the Lord's name in vain was strictly a product of our fevered teenage imaginations, I should point out that our parents reinforced this view by occasionally referring to some respectable-looking older citizen as having the capacity to "swear like a sailor."

All of which makes it surprising that Ross Perot applied to the Naval Academy under the impression that he could get through there and through the active duty the Navy expected in return for his free education without hearing any strong language. I can only assume that the phrase "swears like a sailor" wasn't heard much in Texarkana, Texas, during the time he was growing up there. It may be that Kansas City was a more worldly place than Texarkana; if so, though, how do you explain the fact that at Hale H. Cook grade school in Kansas City I went through the entire Second World War under the impression that Japanese people had yellow blood?

In Texarkana, young Ross may not have had enough contact with sailors to know whether they cussed or not. In the movies of those days, a sailor who dropped a forty-pound shell on his foot would have never said anything stronger than "Dang-nap it."

Even so, you'd think that someone in his senior high school class—some worldly fellow who had transferred in from, say, Amarillo—could have predicted the "moral emptiness" of Navy life that Ross described with such shock in the letter his father forwarded to the congressman who had appointed Ross to Annapolis and to both Texas senators. But it's possible that as a high school student Perot simply brushed aside the warning.

"Ross," I can imagine the new boy in town saying, "I know you have your heart set on going to Annapolis, but I have to warn you that serving in the Navy could mean being in close proximity to people who take the name of the Lord in vain on a fairly regular basis."

"There's not one iota of truth in that," young Ross

says, having already acquired some of the straight-from-the-shoulder bluster that the American voters will one day love. "If you can show me one example of that, I'll buy milkshakes for the entire class."

The boy from Amarillo, still determined to warn Ross of what might lie ahead, says that, from what he is given to understand, sailors on shore leave sometimes engage in acts with complete strangers that the Lord meant only married people to do with each other, and then only if they promise not to talk about it.

"Stuff and nonsense," young Ross says. "Not true. And I have a dozen members of the senior class who are willing to swear that it's not true. I don't have to sit here and listen to some slick Amarillo guy in alligator shoes try to trip me up."

The new boy from Amarillo starts to say he is, in fact, wearing penny-loafers, but young Ross is launched on a lecture. "If there is swearing in the Navy, the way I'll take care of it won't be pretty, but you'll never hear any of it again, I can tell you that . . ."

"O.K., Ross," the boy from Amarillo finally says. "Have it your way."

June 15, 1992

I guess now you'll be wanting to know if I consider myself part of the "cultural elite" that Dan Quayle has been talking so much about.

My Aunt Rosie certainly hopes that I am. Our family has never been part of any elite before, and she sees this as our big opportunity.

"I say go for it," Aunt Rosie told me in a phone call from Kansas City. "If they're giving out some sort of cultural-elite certificate that's suitable for framing, try to get an extra one."

"But Aunt Rosie," I said. "Surely you don't think of me as a moral cynic who sneers at our country's enduring basic values and mocks patriotism and thinks that a family is just a collection of unrelated bozos with kinky habits who happen to live under the same leaky roof."

"You were real smart-alecky as a child," she said. "That ought to count for something." Then she hung up.

Until Aunt Rosie's call, it really hadn't occurred to me that what Quayle kept describing as a cultural elite— a bunch of flat-out sophisticates—might include me. For one thing, I was brought up not to put on airs. Also, I've always thought of the elite as the sort of people who play golf at snooty country clubs and have so much influence that they can get even their dumbest kid into college.

Nobody in our family has ever belonged to anything snootier than one of those video stores that give you two films for the price of one on Wednesday night if you take out a lifetime membership. And when my cousin Elliot got turned down by one of those schools that teach you to be a truck driver in your spare time, nobody in our family had the clout to get him in—even though you'd think a school that was being investigated by both the Better Business Bureau and the state consumer fraud division would be vulnerable to a little well-placed pressure.

Also—although this may sound like a technicality— Quayle said that the cultural elite hangs out in "news-rooms, sitcom studios and faculty lounges," and I work mostly at home. The kids are out of the house now, and my wife is often away at work; on most days, even if I did decide to sneer at our country's enduring basic moral values, nobody would notice anyway, except maybe the UPS deliveryman or the guy who comes to read the gas meter.

It did occur to me, though, that I might know some of the people Quayle was talking about. For instance, I have a cousin who's a professor—he's quite a bit brighter than Elliot; I suspect he could teach himself to drive a truck—but when I asked him whether he was part of the cultural elite that hangs around the faculty lounge, he said he had always avoided the faculty lounge. "There are people lurking there just waiting to put you on a com-mittee," he said. "Also, I've got some sort of allergy so that when I see a bottle of sherry it makes me long for a cold beer."

I also have a friend named Mo, who's spent a lot of time in newsrooms. Although Mo's an editor now, I hadn't thought of him as particularly elite. I've never seen him with the knot of his tie pulled all the way up;

I wouldn't be surprised to hear that when he needs shirts he buys seconds that are missing the collar button.

Still, I figured it wouldn't hurt to try him out, so the Saturday after I'd heard from Aunt Rosie I gave him a call. "Say, Mo," I said. "You want to go down to Lou's Tap and mock family values for a while?"

"I swore to Eleanor that I wouldn't leave the house today until I made some headway cleaning out this basement," Mo said. "Then I promised Jenny I'd help her learn how to use the rollerblades we got her for her birthday, and Tim and I have to finish the birdhouse we've been building together, and then I have to get dressed and get to the plane if I'm not going to miss my high school reunion in Cedar Rapids. How about next Saturday?"

I called Aunt Rosie back and told her that, as far as I could tell, I didn't even know anyone in the cultural elite.

"I'm not surprised," she said. "I always told your mother that you'd never amount to anything." Then she hung up.

MERGER

June 29, 1992

Yes, of course I've been thinking about the marriage of Valerie Jane Silverman and Michael Thomas Flaherty—two fine-looking and richly accomplished graduates of Harvard, class of 1987—who tied the knot some weeks ago and adopted as a common family name Flaherman.

I won't say that I've been thinking about nothing else. We've had half a dozen wars going on, you know, and voters have had to consider the question of whether Ross Perot will get so mad at people who accuse him of being quick to investigate enemies that he'll sic a bunch of private eyes on the lot of them, and Bill Clinton has been trying to hack away with the sharp end of a saxophone, which doesn't really have a sharp end, at whatever strings seemed to tie him to Jesse Jackson. But I've been thinking about it.

I did not need all of those telephone calls asking if I had, by chance, missed the Flahermans' wedding announcement in the Sunday *New York Times*. I stated years ago that the wedding announcements have always been the first news I turn to on Sunday in the *Times*. It has been my custom to do some careful analysis of the family background of each bride and groom, and then to try to envision the tension at the wedding reception.

The names going into the marriage are, of course, helpful to that sort of vision, as is the assumption that every human being has at least one truly dreadful cousin. In an overtly bi-ethnic merger such as the marriage of Valerie Silverman to Michael Flaherty, I would ordinarily have wondered whether Mike Flaherty's dingbat fourth cousin, who has been assuring all of the Silvermans that some of his best friends are Jewish, will actually fall into conversation toward the end of the evening with an equally boorish cousin of Valerie Silverman's who has been poking every Flaherty he meets in the ribs and saying, "I guess you've heard the one about Murphy, O'Leary, and the two priests."

In recent years, though, the name taken after the wedding has added to my concerns. Whether or not the bride is going to retain her last name has become an important element in the announcement—you have to wonder whether the Nancy Jones who announces that she will be keeping her surname after marrying a young man named Cholmondley Rhoenheusch is a committed feminist or a weak speller—and I've been wondering lately whether a wedding someday between, say, the son of Madonna and the daughter of Sting would produce a nice young couple who had to start married life with no last name at all.

The Flaherman nuptials were particularly interesting to me because of the possibility that their approach to merging names as well as lives was the outgrowth of a warning I issued fifteen years ago about the danger of liberated young couples combining surnames by connecting them with hyphens. At the time, I pointed out that if Penelope Shaughnessy married Nathaniel Underthaler while her best friend, Jennifer Morgenwasser, married Jeremiah Christianson, and then the children of those two unions, Jedediah Shaughnessy-Underthaler and Abigail Morgenwasser-Christianson, themselves got married—a prospect that the two old friends, Penelope

Shaughnessy-Underthaler and Jennifer Morgenwasser-Christianson, so devoutly wished that they were nearly afraid to mention it at the luncheons they continued to have over the years, even though such luncheons irritated any number of restaurant proprietors who tried to jam one of those double-barreled names into the tiny space allotted in the reservation book—these offspring would end up as a couple named Jedediah and Abigail Shaughnessy-Underthaler-Morgenwasser-Christianson. Which means that they could never expect to get their name into a newspaper headline unless it was a headline announcing, say, World War III.

I think what the Flahermans—and, presumably, others by now—have done is a resourceful solution to the problem of how modern women can retain their names without creating monikers that make the signature run off the line every single time.

One of the people I talked to about this situation—those of us who are devoted to the wedding section of the *Times* are likely to be sharing impressions of this or that announcement late on a Sunday morning, when people in other households are discussing the trouble in the Balkans or thinking about turning to the breakfast dishes—said that Flaherman struck him as a less euphonious name than, for instance, Silverty, but I consider that a quibble.

So congratulations to the Flahermans. And what if they have a son who wins the hand of Daphne Shaughnessy-Underthaler-Morgenwasser-Christianson? We'll deal with that problem when we get to it.

July 20, 1992

First I read in *Newsweek* that the Garrick Club, in London, had voted 362 to 94 against admitting women to membership. Then I read in the *Toronto Globe and Mail* that the Furness Rugby Union Club, in Barrow, England, was trying to raise money by having female fans bid on the opportunity to take a shower with the team. As the panel moderator often says, each of us must deal with these difficult issues in our own way.

Americans tend to visualize a London men's club as a bunch of old Blimps who doze away the afternoon in leather chairs, waking up occasionally to curse their gout or the Socialists. But *Newsweek* describes the Garrick as a "preserve of actors, lawyers, judges and journalists"— which might make you think that it's less stuffy than some of the other clubs, since actors and journalists are prominent among the occupational groups that prudent landlords in any country try not to rent to.

When it comes to admitting women, I suppose you could say that the Garrick is indeed less stuffy than some of the other clubs: the other clubs have apparently not even bothered to hold a vote on the issue. We're free to continue thinking of the members of those clubs as jowly old coots who are likely to begin their most intimate endearments to their wives with a phrase like "Hilda, old thing . . ."

Before I go any further in presenting mitigating evidence about the Garrick Club, I should probably disclose that I actually know two of its members—startling as that may be to those who assumed that I wouldn't know anyone who belonged to anything more august than an outlaw motorcycle club.

One of the people I know is a journalist I'll call Trevor, and the other one is a law professor I'll call Cedric. I have given them those names to make them sound more like authentic club men.

Trevor was the first of them to join the Garrick. At the time I made an agreement with him: I promised not to make fun of him for belonging to such an institution if he promised never to take me to dinner there. I have always assumed that the chef in a London men's club would specialize in gray, room-temperature meat, accompanied by vegetables that he began cooking shortly after wartime rationing was lifted, and I had no intention of putting that assumption to the test.

Trevor, whose credentials as a gentleman had been confirmed by an official vote of the admissions committee, stuck to his part of the bargain, and I, never having been so certified, did not. Still, I can't think of Trevor and Cedric as people who would cast votes in favor of discriminating against women; I certainly have never heard either one of them address his wife as "old thing."

In the interest of full disclosure, I should also say that I am not personally acquainted with any members of the Furness Rugby Union Club. Like many Americans, I've had difficulty understanding the rules of rugby. To me, a rugby scrum has always looked remarkably like what sometimes goes on in the parking lot after a dance at which the sponsors were lax about checking for bottles at the door, and I know the only rule for a parking-lot engagement of that sort is to try to take your leave before the police show up.

It is tempting, of course, to gather from news of the rugby club's fund-raising device that its members have a somewhat more flexible view of the opposite sex than do members of the Garrick Club, but that may not be true. There is nothing in the news item indicating that the female fan who wins an opportunity to shower with the team will be offered membership in the club.

In other words, the Garrick Club could offer a similar opportunity and still vote 362 to 94 not to admit women. I should say right here that even though Trevor and Cedric have many admirable qualities, I can't imagine that an opportunity to shower with them would result in frenzied bidding.

And how did Trevor and Cedric vote? I haven't heard. I like to think, of course, that they were on the side that wanted to admit women. I'd like to think that, as a matter of principle, they both resigned from the club when it became obvious that a majority of the members felt otherwise. Any day now, I expect to get a letter from Trevor saying, "Cedric and I did the only honorable thing. We resigned. We have both applied for membership in the Furness Rugby Union Club."

August 3, 1992
In the patch of the Maritimes that I retreat to every summer to lick my wounds, there aren't usually many new developments to report, unless the old-timer in town who hands out a lot of folksy but totally ineffectual advice has come up with yet another deeply flawed method for keeping the raccoons out of your garbage.

This year, though, we heard something exciting right off the bat. It came out during dinner with a couple I'll call Ralph and Letitia Jackson, who make the long drive up to our part of the woods annually from the Deep South in order to escape summer heat so relentless that a dip in the local pond could melt the plaster on your bunions. At a roadside rest stop in Tennessee—one of those places with just restrooms and a couple of pay phones—Letitia had driven away under the assumption that Ralph was asleep in the back of the van, and that assumption had proven to be highly unfounded. Ralph, poor fellow, was in the men's.

What excited me about the story was that it was a palpably authentic example of the sort of experience you hear now and then in the sort of modern folktales that usually carry the sniff of the apocryphal and the embellished ("This guy at work knows someone who's supposed to be a cousin of the people this actually happened to"). The Jacksons are real people. Also, they are, unlike the old-timer, thoroughly reliable citizens. In other words, I was in the unusual position of hearing the folktale on first telling.

By the time I heard the story, a couple of weeks after Ralph had emerged to find himself alone early one morning at a place in Tennessee where he hadn't really intended to linger, both Ralph and Letitia were laughing about the experience. But those of us at the dinner table couldn't help wondering whether it had something in common with, say, Army experiences, which tend to seem more humorous in the recollection than they were at the time.

The details were undisputed. Just before the rest stop, Letitia had taken over the wheel, with Ralph trying to sleep in the back of the van. The car was gassed up, and Letitia was determined to drive all the way from the rest stop to the Virginia state line. She had barreled down the interstate toward that goal for forty-five minutes when the telephone rang.

Telephone? That's right. There was a brand-new car phone in the van. Standing at the rest stop, trying to figure out a way to rein Letitia in before she hit the New Jersey Turnpike, Ralph had figured that he might be able to raise her on the car phone. This was after he called the highway patrol, which didn't seem terribly interested in offering any help; they probably figured Ralph for one of those guys who knew someone who was supposed to be a cousin of the people it had happened to.

It turned out to be complicated to catch the van in the right car-phone zone, and when the phone finally did start to ring, Letitia, who was somewhat rattled at being phoned on the interstate in the middle of Tennessee, didn't know how to get it out of the cradle. So she yelled back to Ralph to wake up and get the telephone. No Ralph.

That surprised her some, but she quickly figured out what had happened, and, still unable to free the car phone from its cradle, she stopped at the next rest area. Walking into the fast-food emporium there, she said to the woman behind the cash register, "I think I just did the dumbest thing I've done all day. I left my husband at a rest stop forty-five minutes back."

"The only question left, honey," the woman said, "is whether or not you're going to bother to go back and get him."

Letitia thought this was the funniest part of the entire experience. I assume Ralph had a different view of it, since his response to that part of the story was to mutter, "I guess *Thelma and Louise* has come to the drive-ins."

Letitia did go back, of course. Ralph told me that he doesn't remember what he said when she arrived. That surprised me. He wasn't on the telephone the entire time, after all; he had plenty of time to polish a line. I like to picture him leaning up against the phone booth (about the only thing he had to lean up against) with a toothpick in his mouth, saying, "Forget something, lady?" It may get to that yet. After all, this is only the second telling.

August 10, 1992

My old Army buddy Charlie—who this time of year is hard to separate from his chain saw—phoned recently in a dither over the news that the Environmental Protection Agency is turning its attention toward the air pollution caused by lawn mowers and other off-road gas-powered machinery. "The federals will never take my chain saw away from me," Charlie said. "I'll run off and hide in the forest and live off berries."

"You can't hide in the forest," I reminded Charlie. "You've cut down the forest with your chain saw."

This is only a slight exaggeration. Charlie happens to own an acre or two of thick woods behind his house— a tangled and rocky patch that nobody had ever found any particular use for—and some years ago, just after he got his chain saw, he decided it would be valuable to have some trails through it. "My plan is to cut a trail from the back yard all the way to the northeast corner of the woods," Charlie told his wife.

"Why would anybody want to go to the northeast corner of the woods?" his wife asked. "There's nothing there. It looks exactly like all the rest of the woods."

"Well, just in case," Charlie said.

The trail to the northeast corner worked out so well that Charlie cut a trail to the northwest corner. Then he decided that those two trails would be much more effective if they were linked. After that, one thing just led to another until the woods began to resemble one of those sad pictures you see of a badly bombed city where the odd building is somehow left standing above the rubble every few blocks.

You're probably assuming that my attitude toward this maniacal tree-toppling was concern for the trees or concern for Charlie's stability. Wrong. My principal response was quiet envy. I had some woods that needed trails myself. And my wife had forbidden me to have a chain saw.

Forbidden? Yes, I realize it's an old-fashioned concept. Maybe it's the wrong word. Somehow, though, when the government was formed at our house many years ago, my wife acquired among her portfolios Minister of Safety, and she has always had a strong anti-chain-saw policy. She didn't have to say, "I forbid you to operate a chain saw," just as she didn't have to say, in her role as Minister of Attire, "I forbid you to wear that ratty old jacket." (She could just study me, as I came down the stairs, and say, "Is that the jacket you're planning to wear?")

So I bided my time. I brought up the subject occasionally. I'd mention casually at dinner that a 128-pound accountant we know who's been held back in his firm because the partners find him "too thorough" had just bought a chain saw. I'd muse on the possibility that not being allowed to have a BB gun as a boy, even though all the boys on the block had them, had scarred me deeply—causing, perhaps, a lifetime weakness for beer and sausages. Finally, after about twenty years, she said, "I don't know why you keep telling me these things. I never said that you were forbidden to have a chain saw."

So I got a chain saw. I had laboriously cut some trails already with non-hydrocarbon-spewing instruments, such as a hatchet. With my new chain saw, I figured, I'd be able to triple my trails within a few weeks.

But I had figured without taking into account a joint operation of the Ministry of Safety and the Ministry of Attire. "Are those the clothes you're planning to wear?" my wife asked as I stood in the door holding my new chain saw. I had forgotten the need for safety clothing.

So I got a helmet with a mask that pulls over the face and ear protectors that snap down on the side. I got pants that seem to have every rock I've ever taken out of the garden sewn into them. I got gloves made of steel mesh. I got steel-lined boots that I can lift off the ground if I pause for a beat or two between steps. I looked like the Pillsbury Doughboy.

Also, by the time I got out in the woods, wearing all that equipment and carrying a chain saw, I was too exhausted to do any sawing. Sooner or later I went back to my hatchet.

"A man's got a right to a chain saw," Charlie was saying. "I think it's in the Constitution."

"You can hide in our woods, Charlie," I said. "I've hardly made a dent in them."

August 17, 1992

I wouldn't want to be described as the sort of traveler who sits in the motel room reading the local telephone directory. Still, when I'm in a new place, I do tend to leaf through the Yellow Pages in an idle moment, on the off chance that I might find listings like Metaphysicians or Cat Walkers or Husbands—Removal.

While I was in the Puget Sound area recently, I happened to glance through the Yellow Pages in *MacGregor's Greater Whidbey Island 1992–93 Directory*, and I was surprised at the amount of non-directory reading material it presented. There amidst the listings for Vacuum Cleaners—Household—Dealers and Garden & Lawn Equipment & Supplies were some inspirational passages ("Thomas Edison's Tribute to His Mother") and some articles of the sort you might read as newspaper fillers ("Physical Science Grads Diminishing") and, most of all, helpful advice—everything from "Seven Steps to Better Mileage in Your Car" to "The Prostate: A Common Problem."

I liked the idea that a directory user who might be disappointed by finding no listing for, say, Translators—Farsi could at least feel that the time spent searching had been well spent, since useful knowledge was picked up on how to dispose of hazardous household wastes or how to be a shrewd homebuyer ("Jump in the center of all rooms to see if the floors are springy").

My reservations about this approach to business listings began with an item in the directory called "How to Reduce Air Crash Risk." It said, among other things, "Simple tips include avoiding clothes made of synthetic fibers which can melt on the skin during a cabin fire."

As it happens, I had been strapping myself into airplane seats for years without giving a thought to whether my clothes were particularly meltable, and I wasn't keen to add that to my checklist of items to worry about. For that matter, once I started thinking about worries I'd just as soon not be aware of, I realized that I had never jumped in the center of all the rooms of our house to make sure the floors weren't springy.

In this mood, I came across an article, right next to the listing for Humane Societies, that advised pet owners who have lost pets about how to protect themselves from "false finders." According to the article, "Certain sick crank-callers prey on distraught pet owners who advertise in the Lost Pet section of their newspapers."

Pet owners are cautioned against telling a caller what a lost pet is named or what it looks like. "Even if your pet is a solid color," it says, "ask leading questions like: Does the dog have any spots?"

This was the first I had ever heard of "false finders." I wasn't concerned about being preyed upon by these sick cranks; I don't happen to own a pet. What worried me, for the first time, was that I might find a dog, reply to a lost-dog advertisement like a decent citizen, and be mistaken for a false finder:

"Mr. Smith?" I say after dialing the number listed in the paper. "I have found what I believe to be your missing wheaten terrier. Does his name happen to be Nigel?

I ask because he's wearing a tag that says NIGEL, he answers to that name, and when I say 'Nigel, jump,' he leaps over my credenza."

"I'd rather not say," Smith replies.

"Nigel is not a name to be ashamed of," I say. "People name dogs odd names. I have a friend who once had a Jack Russell terrier he called Full Frontal Nudity—Frontal for short."

"What does this dog look like?" Smith asks.

"Totally gray," I say. "Completely gray coat. No markings. Gray tail. Gray eyes. Gray paws. I would call him a study in grayness."

"Does he have any spots?" Smith asks.

"Not unless they are gray spots that happen to be the same color as the rest of him," I say. "He's really quite gray, your Nigel."

"I haven't admitted that his name is Nigel," Smith says. "Why don't you see if he answers to 'Fred.' "

"Why should he answer to 'Fred'?" I say. "His name is Nigel."

Nigel, meanwhile, is getting so excited at the constant mention of his name that he is jumping back and forth over the credenza, like a gray Ping-Pong ball.

"Fred may have spots," Smith says.

"His name is Nigel," I shout. "He doesn't have spots. His name is not Fred." By this time I am so irritated that I am jumping up and down in place as Nigel jumps back and forth. For the first time I notice that the floorboards feel a little springy.

BROKEN ENGLISH

November 23, 1992

During a recent breakfast at the house of some friends in London, I was forced to ask my host, straight out, what "gormless" meant. I had noticed that one of the English papers, in its American coverage, had described MTV as "the gormless pop video channel."

In England I'm constantly asking what something means. As a result, reading the English papers with me over breakfast is not thought of as a stress-free way of starting the day. Considerate American guests are expected to ask one or two initial questions at breakfast—a question, say, about whether there is some nutritional purpose behind the English custom of drying out the toast thoroughly in one of those little silver racks before eating it—and then keep a decent peace.

In my defense, I should say that I had tried to puzzle out "gormless" for myself by tossing the root word around in a couple of forms: "I'm impressed that MTV no longer falls back on any cheap gorming. . . . The man is completely lacking in common gorm."

I do often manage to figure out a piece of English slang without assistance. The day before, it had been obvious what one paper meant by its reference to someone as the new supremo of programming at ITV, an English television channel that is considered at least marginally less gormless than MTV. (I can pass on that information with some confidence because my host had informed me that "gormless" means lacking discernment or thought—what I believe my daughters would call ditz-brained.) A supremo is what our newspapers would refer to as a boss or a czar or, if the headline writer is in a playful mood, a big enchilada.

Over the years I've had only a mild interest in the differing usages that Americans have traditionally employed to make facile characterizations of the mother country. ("Where else would cops be courteous enough to refer to a lineup as an identity parade and antique dealers be quaint enough to categorize old pitchforks as farming bygones and restaurant proprietors be dowdy enough to include on menus a vegetable dish known as mushy peas?") I do like to keep up with the new slang, though, and on my recent trip I came to realize that I'm falling behind.

Some Britishers might be falling behind themselves. My host seemed to lose a bit of confidence when I looked up from the paper one morning and asked him to define "raver." He thought of a raver as a loud partygoer, although he was reminded by his slang dictionary that the word has also been used to mean a woman who is not known to be overly inhibited ("She's a right little raver"). When I asked the same question of my host's daughter, she left the impression that her father's answer had reflected a certain gormlessness. Analyzing ravers as a distinct subculture, she explained that they often go around in baggy black trousers and sometimes carry whistles and often take the drug Ecstasy during raves and dance to music she doesn't happen to care for ("It does my head in").

Her father had at least been on the right track. I would call him slightly out-of-date rather than ditz-brained. On the other hand, neither he nor anyone else in the family could identify a word I ran across in an *Independent* piece on Sir Nicholas Fairbairn, a Scottish member of Parliament who remarked that some of the women who oppose him in the House are simply "cag-mags, scrub heaps, old tattles." It was easy to get the drift of "scrub heap": nobody wants to be called a heap of anything. I'm familiar with old tattles; I have even been tattled on by a few of them. But cagmag?

I figured it was a term like "sitcom," formed by put-ting together a couple of first syllables that might have done everybody a favor by remaining in their own words. I asked an assortment of Britishers, to no avail. I con-sulted the dictionary of slang, but it was silent on the subject of cagmag. As a last resort I tried the *Oxford English Dictionary*, which informed me that a cagmag is a tough old goose—and has been, at least in parts of York-shire and Lancashire, since the late eighteenth century. As far as I could gather, the opponents of Margaret Thatcher had gone through her entire reign without that information on hand.

While I had the *OED* out, I looked up "gormless," just on a hunch. It was there, along with a citation dating it to 1746. It appears in *Wuthering Heights*. I found all that discouraging. I had been having difficulty enough keeping up with fresh English slang. Now it turns out that they're adding words from both ends.

TAXING THE QUEEN

November 30, 1992

Everyone seemed pleased by Prime Minister John Major's announcement that the royal family has decided to pay taxes. Personally, I can't wait to see whether that trip Fergie took to the South of France was deductible.

I think you could make a pretty good argument to the tax boys that Fergie's little romp, as the tabloids tend to call it, was a legitimate business expense. I say that on the theory that you could make a pretty good argument to the tax boys that virtually everything the royals do is a legitimate business expense. They are, after all, among the very few people on earth who are actually paid for existing. You could argue that when they get up in the morning and brush their teeth, they're doing their jobs.

Some of their expenses—Prince Philip's tailor bills, for instance—are so patently connected with what's expected of the Windsors that they're obviously deductible even under the narrowest definition of royal duties. A personal trainer for the prince would also fall into the category of unassailable business expenses, since a man of Philip's age would obviously have to be in superior shape in order to walk around constantly with his hands folded behind his back and not cramp up.

But then you'd get to some sticky items—divorce lawyers, for instance, and the monthly charges on those cellular phones that the royals are always using to whisper endearments into the ears of people they do not happen to be married to, and the upkeep of those awful-looking little dogs the queen harbors.

Which brings up what seems to be the central question in all of this—not whether the queen can be taxed but whether the queen can be audited. What if she did claim everything as a business expense? Would the Inland Revenue instruct her to show up at some dingy government office with her accountant and all appropriate records?

Somehow, I don't think it would happen quite that way. I think that if the queen got hit with an audit, the tax inspector involved would at least show up at the palace. The man chosen for the job would be the sort of seasoned professional who is called in for particularly sensitive examinations. I see him as a thorough, courteous, monumentally discreet, absolutely relentless man named Carruthers. In thirty years of examining the returns of noblemen and pop stars and other special cases, Carruthers has brushed aside sob stories and invitations to Mediterranean yachting holidays and some temptations too scandalous to mention, all the while pressing onward to wring out every shilling the government believes it is due. His fellow workers call him Ice Water Carruthers.

One problem he'd come up against in auditing the queen can be found on practically the first page of *Titles and Forms of Address: A Guide to Correct Usage*, a book I acquired in England a while back and have held on to just in case I meet a duke over here on a book tour or something: "On presentation to the Queen, the subject does not start the conversation."

In other words, all the queen has to do is keep her mouth shut. It's not just that the inspector can't get any questions answered; he can't get any questions asked. Talk about stonewalling!

Of course, this is why they sent Carruthers. He is a patient man. He might try to wait the queen out—sitting silently and respectfully until finally, bored out of her skull, she says, "Just which figure was it that you wished to talk about, Mr. Carruthers?" or simply "Hello."

But waiting out the queen is no small task. This is somebody who has sat silent through thousands of ceremonies so boring that all an onlooker can hope for is that a soldier faints or a horse misbehaves. She has walked through thousands of factories, listening to incomprehensible explanations of how widgets are made—managing to look vaguely interested, even though the only way she can keep from going mad is to speculate on how in the world Prince Philip is able to keep his hands behind his back that way. She has seen native dances without end. The woman is bore-proof.

Thirty minutes into the interview Carruthers begins to think about that. He thinks of all the ceremonies the queen has to sit through. He thinks of the native dances. Then he thinks of her tiresome children and her hideous-looking dogs. Ice Water Carruthers begins to feel sorry for the queen. He rises, nods in respect, and leaves the palace. Back at Inland Revenue, he tells his superior, "Everything seems to be in order."

January 4, 1993

According to newspaper reports, the idea of Renaissance Weekend, which got a lot of coverage over the New Year's holiday because Bill Clinton and his family were there, emerged when two couples were sitting around and somebody said, "Wouldn't it be great to have an occasion to really share some of your innermost thoughts with some very accomplished people?"

Most people would have an easy time answering that question: "No, not really." When most people feel the need to share their innermost thoughts, they seek out an old friend or a trusted relative, even if that person's greatest accomplishment was a solid 8–6 record in his final year as a Little League coach.

But one of the people present at that conversation a dozen years ago was someone named Philip Lader, then the president of a Hilton Head Island resort, who is described in the newspapers as a "major-league networker." What Lader did, he has recalled, was to organize a gathering of some people he and his friends knew "and others we would like to meet." (The others-we-would-like-to-meet part is the sign of a networker.) Over New Year's holidays ever since, he has brought together people on Hilton Head in the interest of what he calls "personal and national renewal" and assigned them to panels with titles like "New Technologies: Personal Implications for the Twenty-first Century."

Is sitting through panel discussions the way some people want to spend New Year's weekend? Yes. Are some people's innermost thoughts about new technologies? I'm afraid so. In fact, Lader says that this year, presumably because of Clinton's presence, he had to turn away any number of people who wanted to come to Renaissance Weekend—perhaps the saddest souls of the holiday season, wannabe networkers.

This brings up the question of exactly what networking is. If you discount Lader's tendency to describe the people he knows or wants to meet as having demonstrated "innovative achievement on a national or regional level"—and you can put that language in perspective by understanding that Phyllis George is one of the people so described—networking may bring to mind a phrase you always associated with your Uncle Harry, the one who represented several lines of leather goods and was always so particular about the shine on his shoes and the knot in his tie: "making contacts."

I'm not sure it started out that way. As I remember the time when we first heard a lot of talk about networks, they were formed by like-minded people in real need of allies or support—educators who were interested in sharing nontraditional teaching methods, say, or women who felt isolated in large corporate law firms, or newcomers of one sort or another who needed a counterweight to what was called the Old Boy Network.

Gradually the word came to mean a sort of unfocused fattening of the Rolodex. Lader and others emphasize that everyone gets along splendidly during Renaissance Weekend, even though people have widely varying political beliefs, and this reflects a basic principle of what networking has come to mean: it's more important to know someone than to agree with him. Lader, putting it in almost religious terms, talks about "the very sacred value we give to personal relationships." That's the part that reminds you of your Uncle Harry.

So what's the difference these days between making contacts and networking? That's easy. Networking comes with panel discussions. The distinction is important. People who were interested in making contacts were simply out to get ahead. Uncle Harry never cared much about the new technologies—one of his favorite phrases, after all, was "It's not what you know but who you know"— and he wouldn't have claimed that his effort to meet people who could be of use to him had anything to do with national renewal.

Networkers, on the other hand, like to think that they are establishing "personal relationships" with people who share their interest in grappling with what they are prone to call the problems and challenges that face our society—a task that naturally might necessitate their occupying important positions in government and industry and academia themselves.

Lader himself lost when he ran for governor of South Carolina. He now busies himself as the president of what is described as "the only private university in Australia"— a description you'd think a major-league networker would recognize as sounding like a way to say "an Australian university you've never heard of." All this may lead you to gather that there is a limit to what can be achieved by networking, even when practiced at a major-league level. On the other hand, Bill Clinton—who has been networking at least since high school in Hot Springs—was recently elected president of the United States. And Phil Lader knows Bill Clinton.

January 11, 1993

Does it strike anyone else as odd that someone who would have been identified by the local newspaper as William J. Clinton if he had been elected president of the Fayetteville Rotary Club will be known as Bill Clinton as president of the United States?

It strikes me as odd and it also strikes me as unfortunate. I can't help thinking that the further our national politicians grow from the experiences of the general population—George Bush is certainly not the only national political leader who does not have a long and intimate acquaintanceship with the supermarket line—the more they all want to sound like just folks. This is particularly true of any politician who runs for president—even those Washington fixtures who would defect to Albania before they'd give up their car-and-driver.

Jimmy Carter started this nickname business; it should be on his conscience. He was the first president to insist that his nickname be used even for the most formal occasions and the most official proclamations. That didn't make him sound like just folks; it made him sound like someone you couldn't exactly take seriously as president.

The fact that Carter is such a common name made matters even worse. I could imagine some chairman of a

powerful House committee—a man whose gift for keeping names straight had deteriorated over the years—saying to one of the notoriously inept congressional lobbyists
of that administration, "Who? Jimmy Carter? Wasn't that
the kid who used to park cars at the club?"

Before Jimmy Carter was elected, presidents were
known by the names on their birth certificates. When
their nicknames were used by people other than their
friends, it was usually because a nickname fit better on a
campaign button (I LIKE IKE) or the headline of a tabloid.

But Dwight D. Eisenhower is not listed in the history
books as Ike Eisenhower. The previous presidents with
the same first name as Clinton are not remembered as
Bill Harrison and Bill McKinley and Bill Taft. When
Chester Alan Arthur was being introduced from the po-
dium, the speaker didn't say, "I give you the president of
the United States—Chet Arthur." As we are constantly
reminded by best sellers these days, no president could
have been more badly brought up than John F. Kennedy,
and even he knew enough to go by his proper name instead of just plain Jack.

The reason people like Eisenhower and Kennedy
had been christened Dwight and John, after all, was so
they would have a dignified first name if they happened
to be elected president. This sort of naming has long
been an American custom; despite consistent evidence to
the contrary, it remains a central American belief that
anyone born here, even in the humblest circumstances,
has the opportunity to grow up to be president.

In a maternity ward somewhere in the United States
at this moment, a misty-eyed father of a newborn boy is
saying something like, "Why don't we just call him Butch.
I want to name him after Uncle Butch. I love my Uncle
Butch." And the proud mother, gazing down at the child

in her arms, is saying, "No, this baby is going to have a real name, because someday he might be elected president. Presidents are not called Butch."

After Carter left office, there was reason to hope that American presidents would go back to using grown-up names. President Reagan didn't begin the oath of office by saying, "I, Ronnie Reagan . . ." From what I had read about George Bush's mother, who was still alive when he took office, I couldn't imagine that he would have dared try to explain to her that he was planning to sign the first piece of legislation passed during his administration "Poppy Bush." Fortunately, Bush is a name made for a tabloid headline. The tabs wouldn't have been able to use his initials, as they did with FDR and JFK; GHWB sounds like a community development agency in Hartford.

But now we've reverted. Someone I assumed would be President William J. Clinton is just plain Bill. We haven't had a Butch yet, but aren't we headed in that direction? If it's now thought that there's some electoral advantage in calling yourself Jimmy or Bill, why not call yourself something even less formal than that? Think of how much more folksy Buster or Sonny or Bubba would sound. If this sort of thing seems to be working, I suspect that it will be only a matter of time before the proud mother in the maternity ward looks down at the precious bundle in her arms and says, "I want him to have a real chance for the presidency. Let's call him Stinky."

SMOKING INCORRECTLY

On the "Today" show recently, I heard a representative of the tobacco industry express her disdain for the latest government pronouncement on the connection between smoking and cancer—the Environmental Protection Agency's designation of secondhand smoke as a proven human carcinogen—by saying that the EPA was being "politically correct."

"Politically correct" is that rare term which appears at first glance to be positive but is always used negatively. If someone stood up in a faculty senate to say that many would favor the resolution under discussion because it is politically correct, he would be arguing the opposite, using sarcasm that may have sounded a bit less heavy-handed when he tried the speech out on his wife at breakfast that morning.

I first heard the term some years ago, in the conversation of my college-age daughter and her friends, and it was always used ironically. Although they were the sort of young people who were concerned about the environment and sensitive to the feelings of minority students, they reserved "politically correct" for those occasions when, say, the wine bottle got tossed into the regular trash for want of a recycling bin. "Uh-oh—not awfully PC of you," someone would remark. It was not said in a tone that necessitated removing the bottle from the regular trash.

The term soon came to be used by people who wanted to call attention to the possibility that college campuses were suffering from the presence of an entrenched orthodoxy. Some of the people who sounded the alarm were genuinely concerned that, say, a fear of offending racial minorities was having a chilling effect on free speech. Some of the people who sounded the alarm, neoconservatives who had previously managed to keep their passionate commitment to the First Amendment in check, were looking for a semantic club to swing at the left—the previous weapon, "knee-jerk liberal," having atrophied and died some years before.

Since no one claimed to be politically correct himself—those under suspicion tended to argue that the condition did not exist—political correctness could be defined completely by people interested in warning against it. Although it may be that someone somewhere actually argued seriously that short people ought to be called vertically challenged or that pets ought to be called animal companions, for instance, I'm convinced that by now most of the bizarre euphemisms identified with political correctness were invented in the course of making fun of it.

Also, political correctness was defined by those who warned against it as not just any political orthodoxy but political orthodoxy of the liberal good-think variety. Lynne Cheney, a leader of the anti-PC brigade while she ran the National Endowment for the Humanities, was not perceived as practicing political correctness herself when she was accused of rigging NEH panels in order to prevent academics suspected of left-wing sympathies from receiving grants. George Bush, another decrier of PC, was not considered politically correct when his choices for federal judgeships were vetted to make certain that they opposed abortion.

Defining political orthodoxy as exclusively liberal has brought a pleasant bonus to the sort of conservative accustomed to holding forth late at night at the country club bar: he can air the same views he has always aired—views held by nearly every single person he knows—and come off in his own mind as a maverick who says what he thinks, consequences be damned. Clichés about the need for poor people to pick themselves up by their own bootstraps or about the importance of women remembering that aggressive behavior destroys femininity are now regularly introduced with the proud phrase, "Well, I've never been politically correct myself, but . . ."

And if the country club sage does meet someone who has differing views, he can diminish them by saying that they are politically correct. This was precisely the way "knee-jerk liberal" was used: someone who held a liberal position on some issue was supposed to feel slightly uneasy about it because he could be perceived as following a political orthodoxy rather than thinking for himself.

That's the way the woman from the Tobacco Institute was using "politically correct" against the EPA: because a position is "politically correct" it is not to be taken terribly seriously. A nonsmoker who follows this line of thinking to its logical conclusion can from now on demonstrate that he's a free spirit by lunching every day in the middle of the smoking section of his favorite restaurant—as tough and independent as the Marlboro man. He won't have to worry about anyone's accusing him of being politically correct. The only thing he'll have to worry about is lung cancer.

February 1, 1993

I keep track of a president's symbols. I consider this part of my duties. Although Bill Clinton has barely arrived at the White House, I have already begun a list of items that people would mention if they were asked what sort of person he is—a list that now includes, among other things, the saxophone and Big Macs and Elvis and male-on-male hugging.

I've now closed out George Bush's list, which includes horseshoes, pork rinds, golf, Millie, boarding-school friends, and speech without nouns. If Bush now becomes a thoroughly obsessed birdwatcher or a great pastry chef, it will make no difference to the way he is remembered: I have closed out his list. I should note that the George Bush list has no serious overlap with the Bill Clinton list except in the matter of jogging, and, after some discussion with my colleagues, I have decided that jogging and jogging to a McDonald's are two completely different activities.

I've been keeping such lists for a long time now, and I find that there is rarely any overlap from one president to the next. Dwight D. Eisenhower played golf; John F. Kennedy played touch football. Lyndon Johnson ate barbecue and Richard Nixon ate cottage cheese and Gerald Ford ate tamales with the wrapping still on and Jimmy Carter ate grits and Ronald Reagan ate jellybeans.

Didn't Jimmy Carter ever eat barbecue? Of course he did, but it wasn't his photo-opportunity food. A presidential symbol isn't simply something he does but something he likes to be seen doing. Presidents and their handlers try to use symbols to form an image of what the president is, or what he isn't. George Bush's connection with pork rinds and country music and horseshoes and a speedboat, for instance, was supposed to erase the image of Bush as an effete eastern preppie—although I once revealed, in the course of making my list, that pork rinds were always the biggest seller at the snack bar at Andover.

The usefulness of symbols in constructing an image of the president is one reason that presidential symbols don't have much overlap. A president and his advisers have a pretty good idea of how he wants to be regarded, and it has to be distinctive. You wouldn't catch Bill Clinton eating pork rinds—except to the extent that you might catch Bill Clinton eating whatever's put in front of him.

You can see the effectiveness of symbols in creating an impression of a president by trying to imagine familiar presidential symbols attached to the wrong administration. Imagine a fireside chat by Richard Nixon in one of Jimmy Carter's cardigan sweaters. Imagine Jimmy Carter with FDR's cigarette holder. Imagine Harry Truman with Jimmy Carter's teeth. Imagine Bess Truman in one of Nancy Reagan's Adolfo gowns. Imagine Nancy Reagan stopping at McDonald's after her morning jog to have a Big Mac and hug a few folks.

Occasionally a president's symbol is analyzed in a way that he and his advisors hadn't planned. I usually leave such close analysis to others, but recently I realized that some symbols of the Reagan Administration have turned out to be unconscious symbols of the entire era— an era noted for materialism and excesses of wealth. For instance, Nancy Reagan's ball gowns, like so much of what was supporting the glitz of the eighties, turned out to have been borrowed, and not returned.

The presence of jellybeans in Ronald Reagan's office at all times also could be seen as reflecting what became known as Reaganomics: they indicated that, contrary to what your mother told you, it's perfectly all right to eat only candy, you can have as much as you want, and you can eat it any time of day. Poor George Bush—ironically, the very person who had coined the phrase "voodoo economics" for that approach when he ran against Reagan for the Republican presidential nomination—inherited the cavities.

Symbols change. Toward the end of Ronald Reagan's term, he seemed to lose interest in jellybeans, or maybe he forgot about them, or maybe his handlers finally understood the connection between jellybeans and Reaganomics. If Bill Clinton abandons Big Macs for tofu and brown rice, he'll be trying to tell us something. If that happens, you'll know: it will be noted on my list. I consider this one of my duties.

February 22, 1993

"This is an issue that has the potential to split the animal rights movement right up the middle," the voice on the telephone said. "The issue is mandatory seat belts for dogs."

My informant—I'll call him Wayne Marshall—was a bit hazy on the details, but from what I could gather, the argument centered on whether the movement should push mandatory seat belts for dogs at the expense of its concentration on two other issues—the use of animal fur for coats and the use of animals in laboratories for medical experiments.

"How about seat belts for dogs that are being taken to a laboratory for medical experiments?" I asked Wayne.

"Precisely the sort of question that is causing untold divisiveness among those who protect our four-footed friends," Wayne said. "But those questions are only symptoms of the large issues: Where does our responsibility to man's best friend end and an interference in his freedom begin? By mandating seat belts for dogs, are we looking out for the best interests of our canine companions or are we invading their space?"

"I can see that lobbying for mandatory seat belts for dogs would offend libertarian conservatives," I said, trying to get into the spirit of the discussion. "They believe that, to the fullest extent possible, government should stay out of your life, and I suppose they would believe that government should stay out of your life even if you happen to be a golden retriever."

"On the other hand," Wayne said, "how do we know that the golden retriever doesn't want a seat belt? How do we know what he would do if he had the ability to read the statistics put out regularly by the National Highway Safety Council or if he had the manual dexterity to buckle a seat belt himself?"

"And how about cats?" I asked. I was beginning to like this conversation: we just kept asking each other questions, and nobody had to worry about thinking of an answer.

"What about cats?" Wayne said.

"Well," I said, "if it's the responsibility of statistics-reading creatures to assure the safety of dogs by putting in mandatory-seat-belt laws for them, how can we do less for cats?"

"I thought you hated cats," Wayne said.

"In the first place, I don't hate cats," I said. "I'm not a prejudiced person. As I have explained any number of times, I simply haven't yet met a cat that I liked. Also, this is not a matter of likes and dislikes, it's a matter of a just and humane policy toward animal restraint in moving vehicles."

"Cats are small," Wayne said.

"Yorkshire terriers are small," I said. "Pomeranians are small. Is this society now valuing life according to size? Is the safety of a Newfoundland more important to us than the safety of a Chihuahua, even under the new North American Free Trade Agreement? How about other animals that are commonly kept as pets? Do we have no responsibility toward hamsters?"

"It seems to me that meeting that responsibility would require a very tiny seat belt indeed," Wayne said.

"Are you saying that a country that put a man on the moon cannot produce a seat belt for a hamster?" I said.

"It's a question of how best to use the industrial resources at our disposal," Wayne said. "Also, if you must know, I hate hamsters. I don't much like Pomeranians either. They look like hamsters that are overdressed for the occasion."

"Are you saying that you are not troubled by the prospect of a sudden stop by a car carrying an unrestrained Pomeranian?" I said. "It doesn't concern you that a Pomeranian is flying around the car like a carom shot in handball?"

Wayne said that among animal-rights people the controversy over this issue was not really about whether the mandatory-seat-belt law should be extended from dogs to smaller animals but whether human beings should really be in the business of restricting the movement of dogs.

"The people on the pro–seat-belt side—they're called 'belters' in the movement—believe humans have a sacred responsibility to protect dogs," Wayne said. "The most extreme people on the other side are opposed to not just mandatory-seat-belt laws but also leash laws. They say that we now find ourselves as a society with free-range chickens but no free-range dogs."

"And consider what could happen once you go further down the slippery slope of regulating animal behavior," I said. "For instance, mandatory-helmet laws for dogs that are riding on the passenger seats of motorcycles."

"I think you're catching on to how serious this is," Wayne said. And he hung up.

March 1, 1993

Although a former governor of Arkansas has now been in the White House since the end of January, those residents of Washington who are known for always doing the fashionable thing apparently aren't putting goobers in their Cokes yet.

I got this news in a phone call from a friend of mine who grew up in Arkansas and now lives in Washington. My friend—I'll call him Odie—was pretty steamed about it. He said that this is just another example of people in the rest of the country not taking Arkansas culture seriously.

"Also, I haven't heard the war cry of the Arkansas Razorbacks once during the president's speeches to Congress," Odie said. "I thought that when he scored with a particularly eloquent line about how all Americans are going to have to sacrifice to get rid of the deficit, a lot of congressmen would yell out 'Soo Pig Sooey!' or at least 'Go Hawgs!' "

I tried to tell Odie that he shouldn't take the absence of Razorback cheers or goober-clogged Cokes as an insult to his home state. As I wrote not long after the election, Bill Clinton, a man who was indeed born and raised and politically seasoned in Arkansas, nevertheless gives off a mixed cultural signal. A congressman aware of the Oxford influence on Clinton, for instance, might think it appropriate to respond to an effective line in a speech by saying, in a "Masterpiece Theatre" accent, "Well done" or even "Good on you."

Odie ignored that argument. "By this time in Lyndon Johnson's administration, the smoke from Texas barbecues was so thick over the Capitol you would have thought that the British were back to burn the place down again," he said. "When Carter got here, people started eating grits, even though Georgia grits aren't fit for anything much beyond wall spackling. This time, if you mention goobers to these people, they think you're talking about some German congressman from Wisconsin."

For those readers who are in danger of making the same mistake, I should probably explain that people in some parts of the South sometimes refer to peanuts as goobers—a word apparently brought to this continent by African slaves, along with words like okra and gumbo.

In Arkansas, a member of the cognoscenti customarily pours a few salted peanuts into a bottle of Coca-Cola, where they are allowed to bob around for a while before being sucked up and devoured. You might think of it as the Arkansas equivalent of Parisians dunking their madeleines into their café au lait, except saltier. Somehow, it has always seemed appropriate to call a peanut a goober when it is floating in a Coke.

"Well, Coke or R.C.," Odie said when I checked to make certain I had remembered the custom accurately from some of my forays into Arkansas many years ago from Missouri, where we drank our Cokes straight.

I hadn't known, in fact, that Royal Crown Cola was also considered an acceptable place to deposit goobers. "Do people ever put goobers into Dr Pepper?" I asked Odie.

"Not unless they're weird," he said.

Happy to be asked to delve into this custom a bit further, Odie said that, being a traditionalist, he always used Tom's Peanuts, which come in a small cellophane package.

"I guess any brand of peanut would taste good, though, after it got infused with that taste of Coke or Royal Crown," I said, trying to indicate some appreciation of the custom.

"The taste of the goober is not the point of the exercise," Odie said. "The point is that the salt from the goober charges up the fizz and puts a little head on the Coke. It's the same reason that some people shake a little salt into their beer." He seemed a bit put out by my ignorance of something that anyone with a deep knowledge of Arkansas should know.

I felt terrible about the mistake. People from Arkansas can be awfully touchy. After Odie and I had hung up, I found myself hoping that people in Washington do start to show their appreciation of Arkansas lore. I'm sure Odie would understand if they varied a bit from the authentic recipe—Tom's Peanuts in a ten-ounce bottle of Coke or R.C.

I tried to imagine the day when Odie, at an A-list cocktail party in Georgetown, suddenly notices that the man next to him is drinking a glass of white wine with goobers floating in it. He starts looking closely and sees goobers in Perrier water. A few feet away an elegant-looking man is drinking a Stolichnaya on the rocks, and the rocks have goobers on them. "Go Hawgs!" Odie shouts. "Soo Pig Sooey!"

March 22, 1993

Like a lot of people who live in New York, I've been getting telephone calls from friends around the country who want to know what is going on with the *New York Post*, a tabloid that has lately been making even juicier news than it customarily reports.

At one point in the festivities, the editors and reporters of the *Post* published a ten-page spread attacking the competence and character and even mental stability of Abe Hirschfeld, the man who seemed to be their new boss—asking the question "Who Is This Nut?" and answering with such descriptions as "drooling old fool."

For a week, Hirschfeld seemed loath to let a day pass without both hiring and firing Pete Hamill as editor. At the end of the week, Hamill, who over the years has been mentioned in the columns as the escort of people like Shirley MacLaine and Jacqueline Onassis, was for the first time pictured in the *New York Times* being kissed on the mouth, and the person kissing him was Abe Hirschfeld.

What I try to explain to my friends from out of town is that the current imbroglio is simply a colorful version of an old Manhattan script in which real estate sharks and other moguls known for their shrewd investment strategies battle over the right to buy a newspaper that everyone agrees holds all the financial promise of a bad heroin habit.

In New York, no one is surprised to see the *Post* bought by Hirschfeld—a parking lot magnate and sometime political candidate whose best-known connection with the press before this was an incident in which he replied to a question by spitting on the reporter who asked it. Nor is anyone surprised that there are a passel of other millionaires waiting for him to stumble so that they might have the opportunity to lose $300,000 a week.

The *Post*'s tabloid rival, the *Daily News*, is now owned by Mortimer Zuckerman, a real estate developer who also owns *The Atlantic* and *U.S. News*. The owner whose bankruptcy gave Hirschfeld his shot at the *Post* is Peter Kalikow, a real estate developer. Most of the weekly magazines and newspapers of New York have been bought in recent years by people whose fortunes are based on Wall Street money-fiddling or real estate. The man Hirschfeld seems to have bested in his bid for the *Post* made his money collecting accounts receivable.

Of course, newspaper ownership has always attracted rich men. (Among American journals of opinion, on the other hand, there has been a tradition of editors attaining their post by virtue of having a wife rich enough to buy the place. Years ago I pointed out why this could be considered a healthy custom: the opportunity to pontificate weekly tends to make a man full of himself, and this way his ego can be held in check by having a wife who occasionally says, "Get off your high horse, Harry, or I'll take away your little magazine and give it to the cook.")

When the rich men are real estate sharks, they raise suspicions that they're actually interested in the building the newspaper occupies or in controlling an editorial page important to the politicians who decide on building permits and tax abatements. But I think that in most cases the real estate sharks, like other rich people who own newspapers, simply want to be taken seriously.

They know they have always been sneered at by reporters, even though (or maybe because) most reporters are people who, as Hirschfeld often says, "couldn't write a check for $10." A real estate developer who wants to own a newspaper is in the position of the little rich boy who wants to play in the scruffy sandlot baseball game and knows he won't be invited to unless he provides the ball and bats.

Occasionally the rich buyers actually become involved in the editorial product. Zuckerman writes a column for *U.S. News.* I've often tried to imagine the first meeting he held with the editors after he bought the magazine:

"I think we need to find a columnist on world affairs who has a fresh voice," Zuckerman says.

After a long silence among the people whose salaries he pays, someone finally says, "Maybe it'd be good to have someone with real estate experience."

But most of the real estate sharks just want the presence of public figures at their dinner tables and the respect of the down-at-the-heel reporters who have always sneered at them. What they forget is that reporters traditionally reserve their purest contempt for the boss, no matter what his background is. You only have to look at Pete Hamill's expression as he's being kissed by Abe Hirschfeld.

April 19, 1993

A while back, the New York Zoological Society was widely ridiculed for announcing that the Bronx Zoo and the Central Park Zoo would from then on be known not as zoos but as "wildlife conservation parks."

As you may remember, the president of the society, William Conway, said that the change had come about partly because the word "zoo" has taken on an unfortunate secondary meaning. He quoted the *American Heritage Dictionary*, whose definitions of "zoo" include "a place or situation marked by confusion or disorder."

As an example of the secondary meaning overwhelming the first, Conway mentioned the widespread habit among New Yorkers of referring to Yankee Stadium during George Steinbrenner's reign as the Bronx Zoo. He also mentioned the experience of a friend who got into a taxi and asked to be taken to the zoo. "Which zoo?" the driver said. "The whole city's a zoo." Because of fallout from the new usage, Conway maintained, a zoological park now acquires a reputation as the sort of place George Steinbrenner might be operating, even though, in Conway's words, "we're not confused or disordered."

Having been a fairly regular visitor to both the Bronx Zoo and the Central Park Zoo over the years, I can confirm that neither has ever seemed confused or disordered and that neither deserves association in the public mind with George Steinbrenner. I happen to be an admirer of the penguin exhibit at the Central Park Zoo, and I can testify that the penguins, far from appearing confused, seem to know precisely what they are up to.

On a personal note, I have to say that many years ago one of the first invitations I extended to the woman who was to become my wife was an invitation to accompany me to the Bronx Zoo, where I intended to bowl her over with my knowledge of the takin, a hairy beast from Burma that some authorities had identified as the smelliest animal in the world. She was at least mildly impressed, so you might say that I have a bias in favor of the New York Zoological Society.

The society needs some defending these days. A number of commentators have said that its decision to begin calling a zoo a wildlife conservation park was an example of just how far the wacky modern weakness for euphemism can go. But it occurs to me, after chewing on this issue for a while, that there are animal lovers who might think that the zoological society did not, in fact, go far enough. Take, for example, the defenders of the turkey.

That's right: the turkey. In the same *American Heritage Dictionary* that offers an unfortunate secondary meaning for "zoo," the first definition for "turkey" is "a large North American bird (*Meleagris gallopavo*) that has brownish plumage and a bare, wattled head and neck and is widely domesticated for food." Fair enough. But the definitions that follow include "a person considered inept or undesirable" and "a failure, especially a failed theatrical production or movie."

Or how about the gorilla? As anybody who has spent much time in what used to be the Bronx Zoo can tell you, the gorilla is a particularly pleasant animal—a quiet vegetarian that is described in my encyclopedia as "shy and peaceful." And yet the *American Heritage Dictionary* has as its second definition "a brutish man." The third definition is even shorter and nastier: "a thug."

I won't even mention the chicken, which for many years has had the secondary meaning of coward. There are those, I know, who believe that in this case the secondary meaning flows legitimately from the character of the animal—that a chicken is, in fact, cowardly, just as a rat is, as an animal, the sort of nogoodnik that George Raft used to play in the movies. It's true that those nature programs on television never seem to show a chicken ferociously defending her young from an attacking wildebeest or stingray, but I have always thought that laying an egg is in itself an act requiring considerable bravery.

There can be no claim that the turkey is responsible for its unfortunate secondary meaning. The turkey has its faults—dumbness is one; a serious ugliness problem is another; a tendency for its breast meat to dry out is a third—but those faults have nothing to do with, say, a truly inept musical version of *Remembrance of Things Past* which closes after one performance.

So you could argue that the word "turkey," like the word "zoo," has been sullied so thoroughly by a second meaning that it should simply be abandoned. Some might argue that the turkey should be called, say, the wattlefowl. Personally, I would be willing to entrust such decisions to the New York Zoological Society.

April 26, 1993

Like many of his contemporaries, my friend Nick, who graduates from college this year, is unenthusiastic about going out into the biting and clawing and scratching of the real world. He thinks he could afford to avoid all that unpleasantness if Disney would just make one of those heartwarming animal movies about his pet turtle, Steven.

"It would be sort of like *Lassie, Come Home*," Nick said to me the other day, "except that since you're dealing with a turtle, of course, you couldn't wait until it got all the way home."

"I hate to be in the position of throwing cold water on the hopes and dreams of the young," I said to Nick, "but wasn't Steven just, well, an ordinary turtle?"

"Not 'was,' " Nick corrected me. "Just because you don't see a turtle every day of your life does not mean that turtle is dead."

"I'll rephrase the question," I said. "Isn't Steven just an ordinary turtle?"

"A carnivorous turtle," Nick pointed out. "Steven is no salad-eating turtle."

I had to give Nick that point. I remembered that Steven's carnivorousness made him among the best-known turtles in our neighborhood. I should say that Nick and I both live in Greenwich Village, which has many nice qualities but is not a perfect environment for, say, a Saint Bernard. In the Village, a turtle is a fairly common pet. While Nick was growing up, the best-known pet store in the Village was a place on Bleecker called Exotic Aquatics.

Over the years I ventured into Exotic Aquatics a few times myself. That's where the first grade of P.S. 3, accompanied by a couple of parents, was heading to buy a lizard when the little boy whose hand I was holding looked up and said, in a courteous effort to make conversation with a strange grownup, "Are you divorced yet?"

Exotic Aquatics was, of course, where Nick and his mother, my friend Elizabeth, bought Steven. Nick doesn't remember where Steven got his name, although he says that if the Disney people got interested he's certain he could come up with a heartwarming anecdote on the subject. I suspect that the turtle was named after a bologna-sandwich-eating classmate of Nick's at P.S. 3, where carnivores were rather rare.

Nick's mention of carnivorousness had focused my memory of his turtle. In those days my daughters, who are contemporaries of Nick's, had a couple of particularly destructive cats, and I remember that there were times when I used to daydream about feeding the cats to Steven.

As far as I know, Steven never ate a cat—and, in fairness to the scheme for making a movie out of Steven's life, Disney could just leave that part out even if he did. What he ate mostly, according to Nick and Elizabeth, was dried bits of shrimp, which could be purchased in large packages from places that were used to dealing with people who owned carnivorous turtles.

Steven was also known for the requirement he placed on his owners to feed him the shrimp by hand. You couldn't just put some shrimp in Steven's tank; he

would ignore them for days. Apparently, Steven considered the bother of going over to gulp down the shrimp
on his own an option that was not preferable to starving
to death.

It was the constant hand-feeding that finally made
Elizabeth abandon her efforts to care for Steven after
Nick went to college—that and hearing on some nature
program that turtles can live thirty or forty years. Nick
took Steven to college for a while, but he and his roommates eventually grew bored with hand-feeding bits of
Big Macs and Buffalo chicken wings to a turtle. Apparently, it never occurred to them to see if he would eat a
cat.

Finally, Nick told me, it was decided to take Steven
to a pond near a friend's house in the country and return
him to nature.

"But how could he have survived with nobody there
to hand-feed him?" I asked Nick.

"That's the great part of the plot," Nick said. "I figure he must have been befriended by a kindly old fisherman, or a cute little boy who says 'Aw shucks' a lot.
We could work that out with the writers."

"I'm sure you could," I said. "But if I were you, I'd
go ahead with some job interviews. Just in case."

May 17, 1993
At seven o'clock one evening, on the "MacNeil/Lehrer NewsHour," I saw David Gergen and Mark Shields, two commentators I admire, agree that so far Bill Clinton has not been tough enough to be an effective president; they said that nobody in Washington is afraid of him. Then, at nine o'clock, I saw *Lethal Weapon 2*, with Mel Gibson and Danny Glover. I decided that Mel Gibson should be president. Mel would be tough enough.

Here's what would happen if Sam Nunn, without asking President Mel Gibson, started holding hearings that featured a lot of war heroes who, according to their testimony, aren't afraid of an entire battalion of Chinese regulars but would be terrified by the thought of taking a shower in the same room with a homosexual: Mel would sling Sam Nunn headfirst through the passenger-side window of a car. Then he would open the rear door, stick the senator's head in, and slam the door on it four or five times. After that, I suspect, Senator Nunn would be afraid of Mel.

Maybe I'd better stop right here and explain that the reason I'm talking about Mel Gibson rather than Danny Glover is not because I hold with the theory that the country is not ready to elect a black man president. The country is ready to elect a black man president, but he'd have to be a black man who people in Washington are afraid of.

I don't mean afraid of in the way they're afraid of any black man who walks into the convenience store while they're doing some late-evening shopping—even a black man who is wearing a suit and tie and happens to be the deputy undersecretary of labor. I mean afraid of in the way people in Washington are afraid of a president who is tough enough.

Judging by *Lethal Weapon 2*, there's not as much reason to be afraid of Danny Glover as there is to be afraid of Mel Gibson. Don't get me wrong: Danny is tough. I personally observed one bad guy kick him eight or ten times to the head without even raising a welt, and I saw Danny dispatch another bad guy with an electric staple gun shot to the midsection. (After I saw that, I inspected my electric drill—I don't have an electric staple gun—and I was surprised to see that it carries no manufacturer's warning against such usage.)

But Danny seems pretty much in control of his emotions. Mel is out of control, and that's a lot scarier. It's true that the bad guys in this movie killed both of the women Mel loved, and, as they used to say at home, that sort of thing smarts some. But I think Danny would have kept his cool in a similar situation. Mel, on the other hand, emits what I believe could be called animal sounds as he slams a person's head in the car door. I think one of those animal sounds would scare the bejesus out of Senator Nunn.

The senator, after all, is not someone who has himself faced a battalion of Chinese regulars. As I remember, Senator Nunn, the Hill's acknowledged master of defense policy, got his own personal military seasoning in one of those ten-day Coast Guard programs that people used to try to slide into in order to keep out of the draft. The Coast Guard is an estimable branch, but not many Coast Guard guys emit animal noises.

If some of those western senators tried to pressure the Gibson Administration on the issue of grazing rights on federal lands, here's what would happen: Mel would ask them over to the White House. Then he'd beat the living daylights out of them. He'd choke them with chains. He'd stomp on their heads. All the while he'd emit animal noises. After that, the western senators wouldn't think of trying to push Mel around. They'd be afraid of him.

And how would President Gibson deal with a Republican filibuster? I know that from watching the end of the movie. He certainly wouldn't pussyfoot around the way Bill Clinton did, telling reporters that the Republicans were thwarting the desires of the majority of the American people. That kind of talk doesn't make anyone afraid.

No, Mel would handle it a different way. First he'd call Danny Glover, the White House counsel. He'd say, "Just go in the front door and karate-chop a few of those windbags. I'll take care of the rest." C-Span would cover the whole thing until Mel got around to breaking the C-Span camera over the head of the Senate minority leader. After that, even C-Span would be afraid of Mel. Yes, Mel's tough enough to be president.

HURT FEELINGS

Can you hurt a country's feelings? I'm not talking about
provoking a country. You can definitely do that. If you
try to kill our former president, we bomb you; we were
provoked. What I'm talking about is hurting a country in
a way that makes it feel kind of pouty and unloved and
not wanting to do much except sit up late in a darkened
room and sip Scotch while listening to old Dinah Washington records.

For instance, were Canada's feelings hurt when an
internal State Department document that got out to the
press listed fifty countries in order of their importance to
the United States and showed Canada to be only number
nine?

Before we go any further, I suppose you're thinking,
it might be worth pointing out that it was pretty dumb
of the State Department to make a list ranking fifty countries in order of their importance to the United States.

I would agree with you. I would agree that the list
in question was very much like the list you begged your
Cousin Doris not to make in sixth grade—the one that
listed her twenty-five best friends in the order of how
much they meant to her.

You said that if anybody ever came across that list,
a lot of people would be hurt, and a couple of them might

be hurt enough to give Cousin Doris five in the mush. But she made the list anyway.

And just as you feared, the list was seen by Trish Baxter, the snoopiest little gossip in the class, who took great pleasure in informing Wanda LeBrun that Wanda was only fourteenth, four places behind the super-weird Marguerite Waldeen, which meant that Wanda LeBrun disinvited Doris to her birthday party, which was the reason Doris later gave for what she did to the LeBruns' goldfish, which many people think was the fork in the road that set Doris in the direction of being, thirty years later, what her schoolmates often call "the last hippie in Fort Wayne, Indiana."

Unlike Cousin Doris, the State Department has cabinets full of stamps that say FOR INTERNAL USE ONLY and CONFIDENTIAL. The stamps don't do any good, though, since the place is full of Trish Baxters.

The list of the fifty countries most important to the United States was first revealed in a London newspaper, *The Independent,* but I read about it in a Canadian newspaper, the *Toronto Globe and Mail.* I have to say that the first sentence sounded a little, well, hurt: "WASHINGTON—Canada may be first in the American wallet, as the leading trading partner of the United States, but it is ninth in importance to the United States, according to the State Department."

I wanted to reassure Canada, the way you'd reassure a person whose feelings might have been hurt, but how do you reassure an entire country? I saw myself talking to Canada, person to country. The Canada I was talking to did not look like a Mountie or a hockey player; Canada hates to be envisioned as a Mountie or a hockey player. The Canada I was talking to looked like Raymond Massey.

"Oh, don't mind me," Canada is saying. "I'm just

here to provide a market for your tacky manufactured goods and maintain a couple of baseball teams that make it marginally less silly for you to call your little championship the World Series."

"I'm sorry your feelings were hurt," I say.

"Feelings hurt?" Canada says. "Not at all. Don't give it a thought. Well, I'm sure you have better things to do than to pass the time with a country whose importance in your eyes is two notches below Mexico. I'm sure you and Germany, your numero uno, have something planned for this evening."

"You know, we're all quite proud of you for being in the Group of Seven summit of the leading industrial nations, even though your population's less than half the population of France or Italy or the U.K.," I say. "I guess whichever country's number eight must be pretty envious of you."

"I will not be patronized by a country that thinks Sylvester Stallone is an actor," Canada says.

Even in my imagination, in other words, attempting to reassure Canada was not a success. I can't imagine what we could do to make amends. It occurs to me that, just for a start, the State Department could put out a list of countries that are geographically closest to us. Canada would be tied for first place.

IN DEFENSE OF SLEEPING

I saw myself on trial, accused by my wife and daughters of falling asleep while we watch movies on the VCR.

"Not guilty, your honor," I say, but the only reason I say that is that this court does not seem set up to accommodate the plea I'd really like to make: "Even if you could present evidence that I happened to be, in a technical sense, asleep—testimony, for instance, that I was snoring—I have quite a good explanation."

The judge says that if I want to present testimony in mitigation, there will be plenty of time for that after the guilty verdict.

I shift impatiently in the dock. Apparently I'm going to have to stand throughout the trial, like a defendant in one of those movies set at the time of the French Revolution. I suppose this is to prevent me from falling asleep.

If the judge would let me speak, I'd say that for one thing, the movies my family rents aren't noisy enough. If the only noise coming from the screen is people whispering sweet nothings into each other's ears, the sound is the equivalent of the bedroom curtains rustling in the evening breeze, and the natural response is to go to sleep.

It stands to reason that the most difficult movie to stay awake through is a quiet movie. The same is true of plays. If someone who has just arrived in New York with a jet-lag problem wants to see a play, I always look through the paper to see if anything by Sam Shepard is on. About the time an exhausted traveler is ready to doze off at a play by Sam Shepard, somebody on stage is likely to throw a chair against the wall.

This, by the way, explains why my first question about a movie that someone in my family is considering for rental is always "Does it have any car chases?" Members of my family seem to think that this question reveals me to be the sort of thug who likes action movies because there isn't much dialogue he can understand. Wrong. Car chases are noisy.

There's the roar of the motor, the screech of the wheels, the sound of gunfire coming from at least one car. Often there's the sound of a car hitting a wall and exploding into flames. I have never fallen asleep during a car chase.

A man who seems to be the prosecuting attorney is shuffling through the documents on the table in front of him, apparently ready to ask a question. Finally he says, "There was recently a movie called *Raise the Red Lantern*, made, I believe, in the People's Republic of China." He pauses to shuffle through the documents again.

Talk about unfair questions! Talk about bad examples! "Your honor," I say, "this is not exactly your typical movie."

The judge reminds me that this is not the time for my explanations. If I were allowed to explain at this point, I would say that I had concerns about *Raise the Red Lantern* from the start. By chance, it had shown in a neighboring household the previous evening, and I had an opportunity to ask a member of that household—Ezra, who's about eighteen—what it was like.

"Were there any car chases?" I asked.

Ezra thought for a while. "I can't remember any cars," he finally said.

"No cars! There could be trouble. My wife likes those movies made from nineteenth-century English novels—the ones that are mostly people talking to each other in carriages. The clip-clop of those horses' hooves is like the clickety-clack of a train—a lullaby."

"I didn't notice any horses," Ezra said.

"How did they get from one place to another?"

"They didn't exactly go anywhere," Ezra said.

In my desperation, I took a long shot. "Did it remind you at all of *Bullitt*, with Steve McQueen?" I asked Ezra. "The one with the car chase up and down those steep hills in San Francisco?"

"Not at all," Ezra said.

The prosecuting attorney was ready to continue. "Did you happen to see a videotape of *Raise the Red Lantern?*"

I wanted to tell him that in this movie people spoke softly, in a foreign language. I wanted to tell him that this movie seemed to be about rituals—raise the lantern, lower the lantern, raise the lantern—and that the strongest rituals most of us have in modern life are bedtime rituals.

"Yes or no?" the prosecuting attorney said.

"I saw part of it," I said weakly.

It was then that my wife shook me. "If you're going to sleep, you might as well go upstairs and go to bed," she said.

"Guilty," I said.

August 2, 1993

According to figures compiled by Common Cause, Edgar Bronfman was the leading contributor to the Republican Party in the 1992 elections. Bronfman, the chairman of Seagram's, forked over $450,000 in what is called soft money—which may sound like the sort of money that's in danger of melting in your pocket or sticking together in your wallet but is, in fact, regular American cash.

Soft money, in this usage, is money contributed to a candidate's political party rather than to his campaign, so that it's not covered by campaign-finance laws that limit the amount any one person can give to an individual candidate and ban corporate contributions to individual candidates altogether. The softness, in other words, is in the regulation, not the money: the regulation can be bent enough to allow in half a million dollars. If people in Washington were more careful about language, the money would not be called soft money but loophole money.

Despite $450,000 of loophole money from Edgar Bronfman, George Bush lost. There are times—when commentators point out the similarities between the Clinton deficit-reduction scheme and the one presented by the last administration, for instance, or when Bill Clinton complains about the "gridlock thing"—when this may be difficult to keep in mind, but it is undeniably true.

You might think, therefore, that these days Edgar Bronfman is dispirited over having dropped a large bundle in a losing cause. You might imagine him shaking his head sadly as friends mumble phrases like "Tough luck, Edgar" and "You'll get 'em next time, big guy" and "Hang tough in there, Eddie baby."

Or you might picture him as a bitter man, bending the ear of everyone at the club about the incompetence of the Bush campaign. You might picture him saying that he should have known enough to give the $450,000 with a couple of conditions: "Recipients agree not to permit candidate to call his opponents 'bozos' in final week of campaign," say, or "Recipients agree not to make illegal search of State Department passport files in an effort to prove that opposing candidate or his mother might have been spies in Arkansas for the Soviet Union."

Or you might imagine Edgar Bronfman as defiant enough to display an upmarket version of those bumper stickers that say things like DON'T BLAME ME—I VOTED FOR BUSH. His would presumably say DON'T BLAME ME—I GAVE $450,000 TO THE REPUBLICANS.

I suspect that Edgar Bronfman has not, in fact, been made dispirited or bitter or defiant by the Republican defeat in the presidential election of 1992. Why? Because he also gave $100,000 to the Democrats. For all we know, he was in a chipper mood on election night. After all, one of his sides won.

Bronfman was not the only campaign contributor who was generous to both sides. Last spring, to accompany an editorial arguing that the soft-money loophole should be closed, the *New York Times* ran a list of a dozen or so corporations that contributed a lot of money to both parties in 1991 and 1992. The list ran under the heading HEDGING THEIR BETS.

Philip Morris, for instance, spread the money around

pretty much the way Bronfman did, giving the Republican National Committee $406,250 and the Democratic National Committee $152,000. RJR Nabisco and Atlantic Richfield were also in the category of roughly half a million dollars, and they also put their eggs in two baskets.

When I read the list in the *Times*, what came to mind was how it could be used as the basis for an essay question on a national examination for, say, honors students in high school civics: "Some American corporations make substantial contributions to both political parties during presidential elections. In your essay, explain this practice without using the word 'bribery.' "

Is it possible, for instance, that the CEO of, say, Merrill Lynch is simply trying to honor all shades of political opinion among his employees? Could it be that having already decided to give the Republicans $155,200 on the grounds that they're pro-business, he gives $109,300 to the Democrats because one company vice-president who's a sailing freak is wild about Al Gore's plan to clean up the oceans?

Or is this just corporate America's way of making certain that the election-night party is a joyous occasion no matter how the voting goes? I can imagine what the Philip Morris party must have been like last November 3— everyone madly smoking, the television volume turned full blast to carry above those hacking coughs. News of Clinton winning New York? Break out the champagne. Bush pulls ahead in Texas? Cheers around the room. "We win! We win!" the assembled executives shout, no matter what result the anchorman announces. And they did.

August 23, 1993

Friends and acquaintances of the chicken that played tic-tac-toe in Chinatown are grateful to Michael T. Kaufman for giving the bird such a dignified sendoff in the *New York Times*. There have been congressmen buried with less imposing obituaries.

Kaufman sounds like someone who spent many of his own quarters to face the chicken in tic-tac-toe—pressing buttons on the scoreboard to indicate his choices, then waiting with trepidation as the chicken, pecking at a board in a private area of his cage behind some opaque glass, registered his invariably brilliant countermoves.

Standing in front of that playing field, where back-lit letters came on to keep track of the X's and O's and to announce "Your Turn" or "Bird's Turn," Kaufman wrote, "For those of us who have played the chicken, the sight of his empty box evokes feelings of sadness, if not quite tragedy." My sentiments exactly.

When it came to accounting for the chicken's un-canny skill, Kaufman acknowledges the theory of people I have always called The Nitpickers, but he does so in a dismissive sort of way ("So what if its ability to beat or tie us had more to do with the wiring of the electronic game board than with its skill?"). He makes it clear that his sympathies are with those who always believed that this was one smart chicken. Throughout the piece he treats the chicken respectfully as a worthy competitor, in the sort of tone that might have been used by Gene Tunney to comment on the sad passing of Jack Dempsey.

This recently deceased chicken—called Willy by the proprietors of the electronic-games arcade on Mott Street where he worked—had been employed as a tic-tac-toe player for only two years, but was only the latest in a line of tic-tac-toe-playing chickens that stretched back years or maybe even decades.

When I read Kaufman's piece, it occurred to me that I probably never actually faced Willy in a game, since I changed a number of years ago from someone who played the chicken in tic-tac-toe to someone who took out-of-town guests to play the chicken in tic-tac-toe.

Six or eight years ago, I wrote about one of those adventures—taking a Canadian friend I called John Fraser to Mott Street to test his mettle against the chicken. I reported that when Fraser had looked over the situation, he said, "But the chicken gets to go first!"

"But he's a chicken," I said. "You're a human being. Surely there should be some advantage in that."

Not enough advantage for Fraser, who dropped two in a row before eking out a tie. I later acknowledged that the complaint about the chicken's getting the first turn— a complaint made by nearly everyone I took to the arcade—was not the worst response I ever heard a human being make to the prospect of playing tic-tac-toe against a chicken. A number of visitors have followed that with a second comment: "The chicken plays every day. I haven't played for years."

I suppose I've seen Willy play as many games of human-versus-chicken tic-tac-toe as anyone, and I can testify that Willy was professional at all times. Without wanting to be critical, I have to report that this is more than I can say for Willy's predecessor. Once when I was there, that chicken turned round and round in the back of the cage rather than beginning the game, and then laid an egg—as if remembering, just for a moment, that it was not a competition-level athlete but a chicken.

Kaufman managed to solve an old mystery about the chicken's origin. The writer Roy Blount, Jr.—who is known for his skill at crossword puzzles but also happens to be deft at tic-tac-toe—has always claimed that in Arkansas some years ago he met the people who trained such chickens, and that they turned out to be former graduate students of B. F. Skinner, the renowned Harvard behaviorist. I always wanted to believe Blount, partly because that would be yet another refutation of the notion that graduate school is of no use in the real world.

Now Kaufman reports that Willy was trained in Hot Springs, Arkansas, at a place called Animal Behavior Enterprises. Sounds right. But he also found that the firm is no longer listed in the Hot Springs telephone book. Willy may have been the last tic-tac-toe-playing chicken we'll ever see. John Fraser will be terribly sad to hear that. From what I'm told, he has spent a lot of the past six or eight years practicing for a rematch.

September 27, 1993

Not long ago, a friend of mine told me that President Clinton is younger than the Beatles. This was said in the tone of someone offering an interesting but little-known fact, the way I might say, "The largest egg relative to the size of the bird that is laying it is laid by the kiwi bird, native to New Zealand," or "Nova Scotia is completely free of poisonous snakes." Most of my interesting but little-known facts happen to be about animals.

I have a friend whose interesting but little-known facts are usually about medicine. He's the person who told me that the longest hiccupping attack in history lasted sixty-five years. On my bulletin board I still have a headline he sent me: 21 MILLION AMERICANS HAVE NO TEETH AT ALL.

This was sent many years ago. For all I know, the number may be up to 30 or 35 million Americans by now—or, given the cumulative effect over the years of fluoridated water and improved dentistry, the number may be down to, say, 18 million Americans. Judging by President Clinton's performance in answering questions about his health care proposals, I suspect he knows precisely how many million Americans have no teeth at all.

He probably knows how the United States compares, on a tooth-per-capita basis, with other industrialized countries. He may even have some ideas on how to reduce the number of Americans with no teeth or, to put it another way, how to increase the number of American teeth. It occurs to me that this is not the sort of thing that the Beatles would know.

An acquaintance of mine who specializes in interesting but little-known facts about geography turns out to know only two or three facts. He puts them to his friends in the form of questions fairly regularly—forgetting that he asked the same question six or eight months before—and is always surprised to find his questions answered correctly.

"What's the largest state—in area—east of the Mississippi?" he'll ask me.

"I would say Georgia," I'll answer.

He always looks a little disappointed at hearing the right answer, but he puts a good face on it. "That's very good," he'll say. "Excellent. Fine. Not many people know that."

The person who told me that Bill Clinton is younger than the Beatles does not specialize in interesting but little-known facts about presidents. She is not one of those people who can tell you how many left-handed presidents there have been or how many presidents have names that turn out to be an anagram for "sanctimonious."

She specializes in interesting but little-known facts about the passage of time. In 1981 she called me up to tell me that if James Dean had lived he would be old enough to move to one of those retirement communities that don't allow anyone under fifty.

I expect a call from her on the day Dean would have become eligible to collect Social Security. "He and his wife would have been living in one of those ranch houses with the painted pebbles for a lawn," she'll say. "They'd have an R.V. and a couple of grandchildren. By now, he would have started referring to her as Ma."

Even though my friend might have told me about the Beatles and the president as a fact about the passage of time—one of those mop-haired lads could be president now, except for being from Liverpool—you could take it as a way of pointing out how young Bill Clinton is. You could even take it to mean that he is too young to be president—either because people his age do not have the wisdom that comes with years or because their life experience does not encompass enough history to give them some perspective on American society.

"How can we be governed by a man who experienced nothing before the Jefferson Airplane?" people who have that interpretation say. "What good is it to talk about the big picture with a man who has no basic first-hand experience with the music of Perry Como?"

On the other hand, you could hear that President Clinton is younger than the Beatles and rejoice in the country's having a young and vital leader—someone who has the energy to count American teeth.

October 18, 1993

I read in the *New York Times* that Michael Milken, the junk-bond wizard and thief, is now a popular lecturer at the business school of the University of California at Los Angeles. This can be seen as good news for Leona Helmsley, who would presumably be UCLA's idea of an appropriate professor of real estate tax practices, as soon as she finishes up at the halfway house.

Is Jim Bakker available to teach a UCLA school of religion course called "Church Management 101: Imaginative Ideas in Religious Fund-raising"? Or is he still in the slammer? It's not always easy these days to keep up with the academic heavy-hitters.

If you think Milken is on hand to lecture students about how to avoid the temptation to enrich yourself by stealing from your clients and others, think again. According to Francis X. Clines, the reporter who wrote the piece in the *Times,* if Milken is asked about such matters as the six counts of securities fraud he pleaded guilty to, he "discusses Galileo and other penalized visionaries proved right by history."

One student in the class, Art Stanyakovsky, told Clines that Milken is "the smartest man in this country," and another, Scott Ragsdale, said Milken is "a great man—a martyr, not a crook. It's not fair, punishing him simply because society cannot understand how one man could make $500 million in a single year."

This is apparently fairly typical of the thinking of UCLA students who have signed up for Milken's course. Perhaps not coincidentally, it is also the line that Milken has spent millions spreading through the media.

According to Milken's flacks, he is a dynamic and constructive and extraordinarily generous entrepreneur—the victim of envious and small-minded bureaucrats who couldn't stand the way he thumbed his nose at the establishment. Does that sound familiar? It should. It's the same thing they used to say about John Gotti.

In case mentioning Gotti whets the appetite of UCLA's faculty recruiters, I should add that it's difficult to predict whether he will be released from prison before he is the age of a professor emeritus. So UCLA probably shouldn't count on him to do a course in the business school called "Competitive Initiatives 215: The Mob Rubout in Theory and Practice."

From what I gather from the *Times* article, UCLA officials, when asked to explain Milken's presence, point out that technically he is merely an unpaid guest lecturer in somebody else's class—a guest who happens to come with his own production crew and ambitious plans to market the lectures to business schools all over the country. And who shares in the copyright of the filmed lectures? You got it on the first guess: UCLA.

Not paying Milken presumably is supposed to give UCLA what used to be called "deniability" in the Watergate days. Speaking of which, John Mitchell and Bob Haldeman are deceased and would therefore not be available to teach at the UCLA law school's class in obstruction of justice, but John Erlichman is around.

For its share of the copyright—plus, I suspect, some

dreams of largesse to come—UCLA provides reputation laundering. The goal is to give the impression that what lawbreaking Milken did was—as his lawyer, Arthur Liman, explained grandly to the press on the courthouse steps after the guilty plea—nothing more than some technical violations and "instances in which Michael went too far in helping his clients."

That's right: before the judge had decided on the sentence, Liman, in a speech to the television cameras, falsely characterized the charges as trivial. Maybe one of the first questions Art Stanyakovsky should ask Milken in class discussion is the question I couldn't seem to get answered at the time: "If you're the smartest man in the country, why did you put your fate in the hands of a lawyer who could do something that dumb?"

When the judge, Kimba Wood, did hand down the sentence—a much stiffer one than had been predicted—she explained in lucid detail what Milken had done, making it clear that the only difference between him and a common criminal was that he had made off with an uncommon amount of money.

And what is the difference between Milken and other ex-cons? Why is he respectable enough to be teaching at the UCLA business school? The answer turns out to be pretty much the same: he's got an uncommon amount of money left.

THE HOT STUFF CURE

October 25, 1993

I wasn't surprised to hear that the hot sauce people in Louisiana eat on raw oysters is effective in killing a wicked bacterium called *Vibrio vulnificus.* As my Uncle Harry often says, it stands to reason.

It stands to reason because when you eat that hot sauce you know something is going on. This is a different experience from eating, say, a bowl of cereal or a cheese sandwich or an apple. You can feel Louisiana hot sauce begin its work. You're aware that a process is taking place. A whole lot is happening.

Just what, of course, was a mystery until a team from Louisiana State University Medical Center in New Orleans announced the result of some research it had been doing. Before that, there was no way to tell what was going on. If the researchers had come up with proof that the steady ingestion of hot sauce gradually puts a hole in your spleen, I suppose I wouldn't have been surprised at that, either. I just knew it was something.

On the other hand, killing a virus sounds about right. There's a certain cauterizing feeling about the hot sauce when it's prepared just right. Also, now that I think of it, the people I'm accustomed to eating oysters with in New Orleans, all of whom use plenty of hot sauce, seem pretty much free of bugs of any kind.

Most people who are accustomed to eating highly

spiced food take it for granted that there are curative effects. I knew a man in Kentucky who used to say, just before he poured some of his homemade hot pepper sauce on your turnips, "If you've got a tapeworm, this may not kill it, but it'll sure give it a start."

I've always been confident that hot food does more for the body than simply clear the sinus passages. I was persuaded of that partly by the example of my Uncle Benny, who used to pickle the tomatoes he grew in his back yard. It was said that Uncle Benny made the best pickled tomatoes in town; you had to take that on faith, though, because Uncle Benny himself was the only one who could eat them. They were too hot for everyone else.

Uncle Benny was in good health until his nineties. We didn't attribute his longevity to anything particular about the way he conducted his life, but now I realize he was about as safe from *Vibrio vulnificus* as anyone who ever lived. For all we know, every time some of those nasty little things started to nest somewhere in Uncle Benny's innards, he strolled over to the pickle barrel. Powee!

What I'd gathered about the palliative nature of hot food from observing my oyster-eating friends in New Orleans and my Uncle Benny was what the scientists would call merely anecdotal. That is, it wasn't learned from systematic scientific experiments under strictly controlled conditions.

The LSU study changed all that. It showed, under laboratory conditions, that six different brands of Louisiana hot sauce can not only kill the *Vibrio vulnificus* but also inhibit the bacterium that causes cholera. It also showed that ketchup is useless in fighting bacteria. That last finding doesn't surprise me, by the way. When you eat ketchup, you can tell that nothing much is going on.

As somebody who eats a lot of hot food, I was greatly

encouraged by the LSU results, but I'd like to know about even more diseases I'm protecting myself from when I pop a few peppers. Cholera hasn't been much of a threat in our neighborhood. I would welcome a large study that is easy to calibrate. I was going to suggest studying the health of customers who patronize a restaurant in our neighborhood where you can order a dish on a scale of hotness from one to ten, ten being the hottest. It occurs to me, though, that the statistics would be skewed by the fact that one waitress refuses to take an order higher than six, on humanitarian grounds.

Maybe it would be possible to use western New York state, where you could follow the medical histories of people who order Buffalo chicken wings mild, medium, or hot. If you found that, say, people who order their wings mild have four times more colds per winter than those who order hot, the results might be criticized as what the cigarette companies used to call "only statistical evidence," but it would still be a shot in the arm for the six-plus crowd. We'd have a celebratory banquet—oysters, with hot sauce.

November 15, 1993

We didn't do Halloween this year. Oh, sure, I got out my ax murderer's mask, in case I wanted to march in the parade that's traditional in our neighborhood. But we didn't have our usual post-parade party. We didn't hang a witch piñata out of the window. When a friend of mine who lives in another city asked why, I offered a simple answer: "We plumb ran out of kids."

The friend—I'll call him Horace—knew what I was talking about. He has run out of kids himself, and his neighborhood doesn't even have a Halloween parade that can accommodate unaccompanied grownups. A couple of years ago he suggested to his youngest daughter that it might be nice to celebrate Halloween the way they had done in the past, and she informed him that it was not customary for third-year law students to go trick-or-treating.

"That's what it's like here, too," I said to Horace. I told him about how we had to give up our Easter egg hunt several years back.

"But you must have held that Easter egg hunt for fifteen years!" Horace said.

It's true that when our kids got too old to search for Easter eggs themselves, we managed to extend the hunt a few years by having them serve as sort of guides and bearers for some of the younger kids on the block. Finally, though, we had to call a halt.

"Why?" Horace asked. "What happened?"

"Same as Halloween," I said. "We plumb ran out of kids."

When Horace's kids were small, he's told me, he loved taking them around the neighborhood to trick-or-treat. He enjoyed the opportunity to have a little chat with neighbors he sometimes didn't see from one year to the next. It was always fun to see what each child had chosen as a costume—a witch, a Mars bar, Big Bird—and, Horace admitted to me, he rather liked getting into his own costume. He was a pirate captain. He approached each house shouting, "Avast, ye hearties!" If his gang ran across people who offered apples or granola or whole-grain sugarless biscuits or anything other than the disgusting teeth-rotters that Horace thought proper for Halloween, he threatened to run them through.

All that is over now. On October 31, Horace and his wife sit home recalling ghosts of Halloweens past. Even the occasional visit of trick-or-treaters doesn't do much to cheer them up. Horace likes to see the neighborhood kids in their Halloween costumes, but he finds himself so envious of the accompanying adults that it's difficult to muster much cheerfulness.

A year ago his wife persuaded him that he might feel better if he wore his old pirate captain costume when he opened the door to trick-or-treaters, but a little boy in the first group of callers—a four-year-old who was ferociously costumed as a snaggle-toothed monster—burst into tears at the sight of him. Now Horace wears his cardigan—which he was hoping would make him feel like Mr. Rogers but somehow makes him feel more like Mr. Wilson, the grump who lives next door to Dennis the Menace.

Horace and I agree about what's causing the problem for both of us and a lot of our contemporaries. Not long after you run out of your own kids to take trick-or-treating—or to the zoo or the ballgame or fishing—you're supposed to have grandchildren to take their place. There are no grandchildren in sight. When you read about the effects of changing marriage and childbearing patterns in this country—women waiting until after their careers have taken hold before they get married, for instance, or couples living together for years before making it official and having kids—what you don't read about is that this is causing what can only be called a grandchildren gap.

This is why Horace spent this past Halloween at home in his cardigan feeling like Mr. Wilson. He understands that. He understands that twenty years ago someone the age of his youngest daughter would probably have been the mother of two rather than an assistant district attorney. Horace wants his daughter to do whatever makes her happy. He's proud of her. He has every reason to believe that she is a terrific assistant district attorney. On the other hand, he misses his pirate captain costume.

November 22, 1993

There was once a man named Arthur Robinson who was, as they say, very hard to shop for. He was a nice man, but as the Christmas shopping season began every year, his family and close friends and business associates grew to resent him.

Arthur Robinson had no hobbies. He did not grill chicken in the back yard or bake bread, so the problem of what to give him for Christmas could not be solved with a new piece of kitchen equipment or an apron with witty sayings on it.

He had no interest in either one of the big Christmas gift sports, golf and fishing. He did his exercising on a stationary bicycle that was already equipped with a reading stand and a lamp and a radio that had earphones.

Arthur Robinson dressed conservatively, but he was particular about his clothing. For years he had purchased one sort of shirt and one sort of necktie from the same store, and it was obvious that he had plenty of both. One of his nieces had once commented that giving Uncle Arthur a different sort of necktie for Christmas would be like giving Margaret Thatcher a pair of jogging shorts.

He was not known as a fan of any particular kind of music or any particular kind of book. He despised gadgets of every sort. He did not collect anything. He did not smoke a pipe.

"Are you sure he doesn't smoke a pipe?" one of his nephews asked his older daughter in mid-December one year. "I thought I remembered seeing Uncle Arthur smoke a pipe."

"No. No pipes."

"Maybe I could give him a pipe, just in case he ever decides to start smoking pipes," the nephew said.

"You're getting desperate," Arthur Robinson's daughter said.

She got desperate every year herself. "You know, Pop, you're very hard to shop for," she would say to her father every year.

"Oh, don't trouble about me," he'd say. "I have everything I need."

She knew that he meant it, which made her resent him all the more. She often said to her sister and brother that their father was a wonderful person to have as a father until just past Thanksgiving.

Other people who were close to Arthur Robinson felt the same way. When he ran into them during the Christmas shopping season and gave them his usual cheerful hello, they often seemed put out with him.

Also, the huge extended-family Christmas dinner that the Robinsons traditionally had was always dampened a bit when it came time for Arthur Robinson to open the gifts brought by the guests. "Well, thank you very much," he would say as he opened a box of gray notepaper with his initials on it, although everyone in the room knew that he had a thirty-year supply of the off-white notepaper he had always preferred.

Then in October one year, Arthur Robinson made his first business trip to Africa. Having found himself about to return home with some local currency that was notoriously difficult to change in the United States, he plunked it down at the airport gift shop for the first items that caught his eye—two small statues of elephants. Since his business was conducted in a city, they were the only animals he had seen in Africa. They had both been made in Taiwan.

That Christmas, all of his children gave him elephant statues for Christmas. He couldn't imagine why, until he realized that he had put the elephants from Africa on a table in his study. He thanked his children politely, as he had always thanked them for the other gifts that he had no earthly use for.

The year after that, he received nine elephant statues. A lot of the cards said, in addition to Merry Christmas, "For your collection."

Arthur Robinson didn't think he had a collection of elephant statues. He considered asking his wife to distribute that information to his children and friends and relatives. His wife, though, was one of the people who had given him an elephant statue, and he didn't want to hurt her feelings.

So Arthur Robinson continued to thank everyone for the elephant statues—twenty-three by the fourth Christmas following that business trip to Africa. His family and friends had been greatly pleased to find something to get him for Christmas. "At least Arthur's no problem," they'd say as they went down their lists. "Good old Arthur and his dreadful little elephants."

Which meant that when they ran into Arthur during Christmas shopping season, they no longer seemed put out with him. They gave him a cheerful hello. He was always polite, but he resented them deeply.

December 13, 1993

From what I've been reading in the paper, a serious conflict is brewing out in the Pacific because Australian Prime Minister Paul Keating referred to Malaysian Prime Minister Mahathir Mohamad as a "recalcitrant" for not attending the Asia-Pacific Economic Co-operation meeting in Seattle. The remark has been denounced by Prime Minister Mohamad as "this condemnation, this vilification of my person."

My first response to this brouhaha was to comment at the breakfast table that if Prime Minister Mohamad gets that worked up about being called a recalcitrant, he is fortunate indeed that he doesn't live in our neighborhood. I've heard people called a lot worse than that just for not moving along quickly enough in the subway-token line.

In fact, in our neighborhood, the word "recalcitrant"—which, according to my dictionary, means hard to handle or deal with—would not even qualify as an insult, let alone a vilification. I live in lower Manhattan; anyone who wasn't hard to handle or deal with moved away a long time ago. Calling one of my neighbors recalcitrant would be like calling some Wall Street investment banker a capitalist: after you'd done it, the person you meant to insult would still be standing there waiting for you to get to the bad part.

Of course, there aren't any prime ministers in our neighborhood. The closest we come to anybody of that rank, I think, is an older gentleman who is known to some of his neighbors as the Mayor of West Eleventh Street— a title he holds not because he has ever run for office but because he spends a lot of time sitting on the stoop in front of his building chatting with the passersby. From what I'm told, the Mayor is a friendly sort who draws few insults, except from people he has chastised for failing to curb their dogs.

Even if we had someone of prime ministerial rank in the neighborhood, though, I doubt that he'd get terribly excited about being called recalcitrant. Heads of government get called that sort of thing all the time. If Charles de Gaulle got angry every time he was called recalcitrant—not to speak of every time he was referred to as the Big Asparagus—he would have been on a slow boil for decades.

For people in my neighborhood who read about Prime Minister Mohamad's response to being called recalcitrant, there is a natural tendency to believe that he might be just a little bit touchy—like the man down the street who got all hot and bothered just because the newsdealer on Seventh Avenue whom he had asked for change for a quarter responded by calling him a fascist. (I believe the gentleman in question now lives in Rye. The newsdealer is still on Seventh Avenue, and getting testier.)

This interpretation of personal touchiness is undercut, though, by the fact that the entire government of Malaysia seems to be up in arms about the prime minister's having been called a recalcitrant. In the *New York Times* account of the wrangle, the Malaysian foreign minister, Abdullah Ahmad Badawi, is quoted as saying that Prime Minister Keating's remarks went "beyond extreme."

The Malaysian government is riled enough to say that if the prime minister doesn't get a proper apology from Prime Minister Keating, Malaysia might reduce its diplomatic relations with Australia and start a boycott of Australian goods—no small matter, since Malaysia represents a hefty market that has been increasing its Australian imports at the rate of fourteen percent a year.

According to the *Times*, in fact, "Diplomats from other Asian governments are quietly lining up behind Dr. Mahathir, saying that Mr. Keating's remarks were unnecessarily rude and showed that Australia's leaders, used to name-calling in their domestic politics, are still not ready to operate among the nonconfrontational societies of Asia."

The problem, then, is cultural. I hadn't thought of Asian societies as nonconfrontational—Pearl Harbor comes to mind as an example to the contrary—but according to an Asian diplomat quoted in the *Times*, "In this part of the world, attacks cannot be personal."

If all this is cultural, that explains why people in our neighborhood find Prime Minister Mohamad's anger puzzling. As far as I know, there are no Malaysians living in the area. Someday, though, we'll probably have a few— one of the things I like about my neighborhood is that everyone is welcome—and now I know not to be personally confrontational with them.

If a Malaysian is dawdling in the subway-token line, I'll say, without looking at anyone, "Since some people here are concerned about being late for work, it might be better for all if this line moved more rapidly." Also, I'd suggest that they avoid the newsdealer on Seventh Avenue.

December 20, 1993
Could it be that about a year ago, under the impression
that I was writing about something else, I predicted the
appointment of the White House's new deputy chief of
staff?

It's possible. One of the dismal truths of political life
in this country is that the people who gravitate to Washington are so predictable that a commentator on the
events of the day often finds himself accidentally clair-
voyant. This relentless predictability accounts for the re-
silience of the American political phrase "Here they go
again."

About a year ago I wrote about Renaissance Weekend, the annual strivers' convention on Hilton Head Island which the Clintons always attend. I mentioned what
Renaissance Weekend types call networking, which, I explained, is more or less what your Uncle Harry (the one
who represented several lines of leather goods and was so
particular about the shine on his shoes) used to describe
as making contacts, except that panel discussions are
added. In other words, despite the fact that these people
can go on about The Challenges That Face Our Society
until you want to run shrieking from the room, they are
basically believers in your Uncle Harry's favorite dictum:
"It's not what you know, it's who you know."

The organizer of Renaissance Weekend, Philip

Lader, was described in press reports as a "major-league networker." But I pointed out that all his networking had landed him only the presidency of what was described as "the only private university in Australia."

That description—"the only private university in Australia"—reminded me of something, and a few months later I finally remembered what it was. Years ago, we used to refer to Linardi's Laundromat "as the only alliterative Italian laundromat in the West Village." It was a distinction that didn't have much effect on how the towels were done.

Although I took Philip Lader's position as an indication that there were limits to what even major-league networking could accomplish, I ended the column by saying, "On the other hand, Bill Clinton—who has been networking at least since high school in Hot Springs—was recently elected president of the United States. And Phil Lader knows Bill Clinton."

As a student of French might say if he had the advantage of having attended a private university below the equator, *voilà!* Just about a year after I wrote that column, the White House announced that the new deputy chief of staff would be Philip Lader.

At the same moment I learned that he hadn't been spending the previous year as the president of the only private university in Australia. He had already been given one government job, at the Office of Management and Budget. I couldn't help wondering whether we taxpayers had to bear the cost of having his Rolodex shipped back from Australia.

And what created the hole in the White House staff that Lader was brought in to fill? The deputy chief of staff and the head of the congressional liaison office— two powerful aides of a president who had promised to end the revolving door that allowed people to move "from public service to private enrichment"—had left to take cushy jobs as chief executive officers of organizations that lobby the government. Not surprisingly, the phrase "Here they go again" was heard in the land.

Unfairly, said the White House. The Clinton Administration's rules on these matters prevent someone from lobbying the agency he just left, but not from becoming the boss of the people who lobby the agency he just left. Claiming that the administration established rules that are stricter than anything that existed in the past, George Stephanopoulos said the criticism was "proof of the old adage that no good deed goes unpunished."

One of the most predictable things about White House aides who have suddenly become famous, aside from the fact that they tend to start dating movie stars, is that they love to hear themselves utter sound bites that turn out to be just a bit off the point. The adage that actually applies in this case is the Washington version of the one Stephanopoulos mentioned: "No good deed goes without a loophole."

The same commentators who criticized the use of the loophole also criticized the appointment of Lader on the grounds that he has little experience in Washington and none in national politics. They're assuming that someone is appointed to such a position because of what he knows. They didn't listen carefully enough to Uncle Harry.

January 10, 1994

This was toward the end of a long bout of what I'd finally diagnosed as the 192-hour flu. My wife was on her first day of jury duty, and I had been housebound alone all day, coughing and sneezing and blowing my nose. Not a lot had happened. I think I can honestly say the most exciting thing that had happened all day was a wrong number.

The caller was somebody who had been trying to dial his veterinarian, to talk about this skin condition his cat had developed around the paws. We chatted about it for a while. His cat's name is Elvira. She doesn't seem particularly aware of the skin condition, but her owner finds it worrisome anyway. I'm not ordinarily interested in either cats or skin conditions, but it was a break in the day.

About five, I heard my wife's key in the door. I was going to get a report from the outside world—the most exciting turn of events since the skin-condition call. My expectations were modest. I was hoping maybe she had run into a friend and collected a little gossip or that there had been an interesting argument in the subway or that a citizen who slipped on the ice had been righted by an alert Airedale.

You can imagine my excitement when my wife reported that she had actually been selected for a criminal jury and was already beginning to hear a case. "Tell me all about it," I said. "I want to hear every detail—the charge, the look on the alleged malefactor's face, the obvious holes in the opening statements. I want to know about the sighs from your fellow jurors showing disbelief at something the prosecutor or the defense attorney said. I'm interested in where you see tension developing in the jury room when the time for deliberation comes. If you see yourself in the Henry Fonda role—gradually, through quiet logic, bringing the jury around to acquit this innocent lad—don't be afraid to say so. Spare me nothing."

"The judge said we're not supposed to discuss the case with anybody," my wife said.

"But I'm sure he didn't mean spouses," I said. "I'm sure the judge, a representative of authority in this society that is based on the rule of law, has no interest in erecting barriers that block communication between two lawfully wedded human beings—two people who have taken vows of marriage in which they promise to share the bitter with the sweet and hold back nothing from each other."

"He specifically mentioned spouses as among the people we weren't supposed to talk to about the case," she said.

I thought about that for a while. Finally I said, "I would be willing to tell you everything that happened on C-Span today. I'm talking about the juicy parts, now. I'm talking about the total story on the Banking Committee's hearings on long-term debentures. The works."

"I appreciate the offer," she said, "but I think you told me about that yesterday. It sticks in my mind because I remember that the part about long-term debentures went on pretty long."

I thought about what other morsel from my day I had to offer my wife as a bit of pump priming for some inside information on her case. Aside from C-Span, about all I could remember from television was a variety of cold-remedy commercials.

As far as I could tell, there is a competition going on among pharmaceutical manufacturers on the question of how many hours of relief their cold remedies offer. Most of the commercials seemed to show people rejecting something that offered only, say, six hours of relief in favor of something that offered twelve hours of relief, or rejecting something that offered twelve hours of relief for something that offered twenty-four hours of relief. Nothing offered 192 hours of relief.

"Did we discuss cold-remedy commercials yesterday?" I asked as dinner was being prepared.

"Yes, we did," she said. "I remember thinking when we went to sleep that I was about to get eight hours of relief from discussing cold-remedy commercials."

"Something I've always wondered is whether jurors find themselves trying to search the face of the defendant who's been accused of a violent crime to see if he really looks violent," I said. "Assuming he's accused of a violent crime, like armed robbery or even murder."

"I didn't say it was a violent crime," my wife said as we brought the food to the table. "The judge told us not to discuss it."

I didn't say anything for a while. Then I said, "I like this soup."

My wife nodded. "Well," she said, "tell me about your day."

January 24, 1994

A day or two after the Webers' son—Jeffrey, aged twenty-six—finally moved out of the house, they realized that they had lost the ability to tape. I heard about this from my friend Horace, who seems to specialize in stories about our contemporaries—people who are in that awkward phase between the end of paying tuition and the beginning of playing with grandchildren. Very few of those people are much good with a VCR.

Until Bennett and Linda Weber discovered the effect Jeffrey's move had on their taping operation, Horace told me, they had been pleased by his departure. It wasn't that they weren't fond of Jeffrey, who had always been a bright and sweet-tempered boy. It was simply that, as Linda Weber put it, "if Jeffrey's going to find himself, it would probably help to look somewhere other than his own room."

Jeffrey, who sometimes worked as a technician for avant-garde theater productions, had moved into a cheap railroad flat found by his college friend Jason, who was clerking at a record store as a way of supporting himself while he carried on what he referred to as his true life's work—trying to decide whether to go on to graduate school. Helen, the third roommate, was working as a waitress while she took acting lessons, although she made it clear that the object of the lessons was never a career in the theater.

Since not just Jeffrey but all three roommates were sometimes described as trying to find themselves, Bennett Weber referred to them collectively as The Lost Patrol, the name of his favorite old Victor McLaglen movie—which was, ironically, the movie he was about to copy off one of the cable channels until he realized that Jeffrey was the only person in the family who knew how to tape from the excruciatingly complicated cable box.

"I had a lot of sympathy with his predicament," Horace said. "I don't know if you've ever tried taping off one of those cable boxes without a kid around, but it's no joke. The other night I figured I'd tape *Charade*, with Cary Grant and Audrey Hepburn, and I found myself trying to hold three different remote-control gizmos, plus the instructions. I finally put everything down and called my daughter in Phoenix."

I counted my blessings: I have a daughter who lives just around the corner. "So what did Weber do?" I asked.

"He called Jeffrey, of course, who said something like, 'How do you expect to grow up to be an independent human being if you can't even get along without your son for three days?' Then he printed out instructions for taping that even Bennett can understand, and took them over there. Jeffrey's O.K. I wouldn't call him highly motivated, but he's O.K."

"If he has an extra copy of those instructions, I wouldn't mind seeing it," I said. "Just out of curiosity."

"The next time Bennett called Jeffrey," Horace continued, "Jeffrey said, 'What happened, Pop? You lose the instructions and now there's a Lawrence Welk retrospective you want to save for posterity?' The kid's clever. Anyway, that wasn't the problem at all. The problem was that the Webers' answering machine got unplugged, and

Bennett didn't know how to reset the access mechanism."

"I think there's a little thing in the back," I mumbled. "The last time that happened to ours, my daughter happened to be home using the washer-dryer, so naturally . . ."

"So Jeffrey went right over and reset the access mechanism," Bennett said. "And while he was there, he showed Bennett how to set the alarm on his digital watch, which had gone off right in the middle of the best action scene of *The Lost Patrol.* Bennett can now do it himself perfectly."

"It sounds like Jeffrey may have a gift for helping pre-microchip people survive," I said.

"Exactly what Bennett and Linda thought," Horace said. "And out of that came Jeffrey's company—TechnoKlutz Ltd. He does an in-home course on how to work your machines. Most of his customers are people whose kids have just moved out. He's doing so well he might franchise."

"The Webers must be proud of him," I said.

"They are," Horace said. "In fact, Linda told him that a big executive like him shouldn't be living in a crummy railroad flat. She's hoping that he'll move back home."

OUT OF STYLE

February 14, 1994

The Stamps, Coins and Camera columns
have been discontinued.
—*Notice in the* New York Times,
Sunday, January 2, 1994

Just like that. Gone. Vaporized. The next Sunday it was
if they had never been there. A reader who had returned
from a few weeks out of town might have assumed, as
he leafed through the trendy new Styles section looking
for tips on how to acquire the mannerisms of an in-the-
know teenager, that the authors of three columns—
Stamps, Coins, Camera—had fallen ill at once, struck
down by some odd virus that affects only obsessive
hobbyists.

According to an accompanying notice, Chess and
Bridge will continue to appear on certain weekdays but
are no longer part of the Sunday paper. Apparently, the
back pages of the Styles section will now be given over
completely to weddings. It's as if those hip kids who run
the weekly Friday Night Sock Hop had persuaded the
principal that permitting the wonks of the Chess Team
and the Stamp Club to hang around for meetings on the
same evening just ruins everybody's fun.

As it happens, I have no interest in stamps, coins,

cameras, chess, or bridge. My only hobby is reading the wedding announcements in the Sunday *Times*. Over the years, I've developed the same sort of skill in making small distinctions in the backgrounds of the bride and groom that stamp collectors make in various Luxembourg commemoratives. I know the pecking orders of schools and suburbs; I know which debutante parties can be bought into and which are authentically snotty; I know where the fissures run between and within ethnic groups. I long ago acknowledged the source of my interest: I enjoy contemplating the sort of tensions that are likely to come out at the reception. You think that's a mean-spirited basis for a hobby? There are coin collectors whose motives are not so pure either.

Given my own interests, you might think the *Times* announcement would cause me to celebrate—to treat myself to some champagne and the sort of hors d'oeuvres one might find at the wedding of a Greek-American Columbia Law School graduate from Ozone Park to an intern whose B.A. is from Yeshiva. That might have been my response, in fact, if it hadn't been for my childhood friend Herbert.

For many years Herbert has read the Sunday *Times* almost exclusively for its coverage of coins, stamps, and cameras. I say almost because if he had a little extra time on his hands, it was his custom to peruse the chess and bridge columns as well.

"Chess is still going to be in the paper on Tuesdays," I said to Herbert when I reached him on the telephone shortly after I read the announcement. "You'll be able to catch the bridge column five days a week—just not on Sunday."

"Thanks," Herbert said, without enthusiasm. "It's nice of you to say so."

"Herbert," I said, "you can't take this personally. It's

not as if the editors of the *Times* got together and decided that there's a certain sort of reader they don't want to have around on Sundays."

I felt I had to say that because, frankly, Herbert has always had a little problem in the self-esteem department. Some of his friends think it dates right back to the time when the principal asked the Chess Team and the Stamp Club to move their meetings to Thursday nights for some trumped-up reason that everybody knew was a cover for the distaste of the Sock Hop crowd. Herbert was recording secretary of the Stamp Club that year.

"I guess there's no chance of my letter getting in now," Herbert said, referring to a letter he'd written to the stamps column about a Nicaraguan airmail stamp he passionately felt was underappreciated.

"Maybe the chess column would run it on a slow Tuesday," I said, grasping at straws.

"No, it's gone," Herbert said.

He's right, of course. On Sunday mornings now, I can picture Herbert in his favorite armchair. The Styles section, featuring a front-page piece on whether the fashion of wearing navel rings has played itself out, lies unread at his feet. He's staring out into space.

Given that picture in my mind, it's difficult for me to conjure up wedding receptions. I still read the announcements—actually, I've been looking for something that might pique Herbert's interest, such as the son of a noted coin collector hitching up with the associate editor of a stamp magazine—but often on Sunday mornings I stare out into space myself.

March 7, 1994

News that a courier at the Rose law firm has testified to the shredding of documents relevant to the Whitewater case brings to mind a saying I've heard credited to Jack Valenti, once a close advisor to Lyndon Johnson, on the secret of having a successful career in Washington: "Do your own Xeroxing."

If Winston Churchill, who was even more eloquent than Jack Valenti, were still on the scene to toss around a phrase he made famous during the Second World War—"soft underbelly," as in attacking the Axis powers in their soft underbelly—he might have by now referred to the office copying machine as the soft underbelly of Washington power.

As it turns out, of course, modern technology has given Washington more than one soft underbelly. On the table next to the copier is its dangerous mirror image, the shredder. Next to that are the dictating machine and the tape recorder—those newfangled instruments that American political figures, to their ultimate sorrow, can never seem to get the hang of.

The modern office machinery for disseminating or destroying information provides what someone of Churchillian inclination might call a two-edged sword: its power is awesome, but its operation usually requires a potential witness. For those of us who often find ourselves baffled by technology, one of the most poignant scenes conjured up by the Watergate investigation was a vision of what Richard M. Nixon, a man who had always left hand–eye coordination to others, would have looked like trying to erase eighteen and a half minutes of tape-recording on his own.

Ask Senator Robert Packwood, that unfortunate gold medalist in the one-man lunge, about the perils of employing people to operate such instruments. The day before the news about the Whitewater shredding came out, Chief Justice William Rehnquist ruled that the senator's personal diaries were indeed evidence that the Senate Ethics Committee had a right to see in its investigation of his conduct. "Whatever merit applicant's argument may have had initially, it has been seriously undermined by the evidence presented to the District Court, that his diary transcripts and tapes have been altered," the chief justice said.

And how did such evidence find its way to the District Court? Through the testimony of someone described as an aide to the senator—someone accustomed to working such machines as tape recorders and word processors.

Of course, if Senator Packwood had recorded his innermost thoughts in the manner of a United States senator of, say, the early eighteenth century—spending solitary evenings next to a dim oil lamp, scratching with a quill pen on foolscap—he would never have been able to amass what he himself has estimated as 8,500 single-spaced pages. On the other hand, the entire diary could have been disposed of during a quiet evening in front of the fireplace, with no one the wiser.

I have to say that after listening to Senator Packwood being interviewed by Barbara Walters on "20/20," my heart goes out to the staff attorneys of the Senate

Ethics Committee who have to go through 8,500 pages of his innermost thoughts, but that's beside the point. The evidence is voluminous and potentially devastating. You could say that Senator Packwood has been hoisted by his own petard, except that it's difficult to see how something as palpably undigitalized as a petard would be available in a United States senator's office.

The verdict is still out on whether the shredder will prove to be for Oliver North the soft underbelly that all marines are philosophically committed not to acquire. North and Fawn Hall, the Vanna White of office machinery, shredded a lot of evidence as agents closed in on the Reagan Administration's arms-for-hostages caper—an arrangement that, I suspect, is still referred to fondly in Iran by a Farsi phrase that translates roughly as "the time we snookered the yahoos."

North, though, says he's proud to have shredded the evidence—so proud that you'd think that the agents closing in on him were from the KGB or maybe Hamas. Alas, they were from the FBI, which sort of spoils the story.

The voters of Virginia will eventually decide whether North emerged unscathed from his brush with office machinery. It seems clear that even if Packwood manages to last out his term, his days of winning elections are over. Nixon's herculean efforts to rehabilitate himself are tripped up regularly by a new release of transcripts from that infernal machine.

And Jack Valenti? He has thrived as the mouthpiece for the motion picture industry. I can picture him now—a natty man working in a vast and impressive office. He is standing at a Xerox machine.

March 14, 1994
If I'm watching a movie and something happens in the movie that could never happen in real life, I may express some irritation. This probably doesn't come as a complete surprise to you.

Some years ago, after all, I acknowledged that I have been known to shout at the television set when something happens in a television drama that would never happen in real life. I admitted, in fact, that my wife had threatened to banish me to another room during "L.A. Law," which we used to watch on the bedroom television set, if I didn't quit leaping to my feet during implausible courtroom scenes and shouting, "Objection, your honor!"

"I thought we decided that you weren't going to stand on the bed to make objections during 'L.A. Law,' " my wife would say.

"But that lawyer is not allowed to do that in cross-examination," I'd say. "No judge would allow him to do that."

"It doesn't make any difference," my wife would say. "Nobody cares about that sort of thing."

"I care," I would say. "I care deeply."

If you remembered that I tend to shout at the television set during moments of blatant impossibility, the only question you might have had about my response to movies was whether it is less demonstrative, considering the fact that a movie theater is a public place. You probably guessed the answer to that one, too: no.

I hate it when characters in movies behave in a way they wouldn't really behave; I'm constantly on guard for inaccuracies and anachronisms. I'm the guy in the movie theater who's always saying things like "That word wasn't used in 1942" or "No police detective would ever do that." My wife is the person next to me saying "Shhhh."

When some truly unbelievable plot turn is being set up or when someone is being rendered unconscious but unbruised by a friendly right to the jaw ("I'm sorry to have to do this," the puncher says just before the punch) or when someone is driving a car at eighty miles an hour over cornfields, I'm the one in the theater you hear emitting a loud sigh. Actually, it's a loud sigh if I happen to be on my best behavior. More often, it's a mumbled "Gimme a break" or even a clearly audible "Get serious!"

When *Philadelphia* came out, my wife and I went to see it at our neighborhood movie house. Although *Philadelphia* is an admirable attempt to discuss the AIDS epidemic through the personal story of one human being, a young corporate lawyer in Philadelphia, its courtroom scenes make the courtroom scenes in "L.A. Law" look like a demonstration workshop sponsored by the American Bar Association's committee on litigation techniques.

After a while, every time the movie got back to the courtroom I would be asked by the people behind me to sit down: I had been halfway to my feet, prepared to object. I always resumed my seat with a quick but polite apology. I did not turn to explain that a lawyer who is examining a witness is not permitted to make speeches rather than ask questions. That's right: I do everything I can to prevent these incidents from turning nasty.

Nobody likes having a flashlight shined in his eyes

by some officious usher who is saying, "Sir, I'll have to ask you to be quiet so that others may enjoy the film." But I always resist the temptation to reply, "I'll have to ask you to show films that do not depict people driving automobiles in a manner that defies the laws of physics."

Most important, I try to avoid the incidents in the first place by not going to movies that I know are going to bring me to my feet on a regular basis. For instance, I don't go to movies featuring any character who is in the wrong body or the wrong century or the wrong solar system.

That's right. If a character in a movie I'm expected to watch dies, he is required to remain dead. He isn't allowed to come back as an invisible spirit so he can look after his wife and kids when they're in danger. He can't remain frozen for thirty or forty years and then get thawed out accidentally by some oversized microwave. He isn't permitted to wander off to some other century or return to earth as a golden retriever. Dead is dead.

Dead or alive, he's not allowed to change bodies. Everyone is required to end the movie in the same body he came in in. Members of the audience are not allowed to be in the movie. Ghosts are out, also angels. I know that eliminates a few distinguished movies—It's a Wonderful Life, for instance—but a rule's a rule.

DIN! DIN! DIN!

March 21, 1994
A devotion to *Gunga Din* is an awkward thing to bring
to a marriage. This has been particularly true since some
Americans began to take movies seriously—I put the date
of that sometime in the spring of 1956—and your favorite
movie became less like your favorite ice cream flavor than
like a test of your character. When my wife and I got
married, in 1965, I wouldn't have been surprised to hear
that her friends were speculating about how long she'd
be able to remain in a union with somebody who was
filmicly stunted.

My father brought me up to believe that *Gunga Din*
was the greatest movie ever made, in the way some fath-
ers brought up their sons to seek revenge for the Battle
of the Boyne. To this day I'm enthralled by the roistering
sergeants, Cary Grant and Victor McLaglen and Douglas
Fairbanks, Jr. I laugh out loud every time I see my father's favorite scene: During a brawl, Cary Grant is about
to slug a man he is holding halfway out a second-story
window. A nonroistering sergeant on the street shouts
up, "Take your hands off that man!" Grant, obeying orders for once, removes his hands and lets the man fall to
the street below.

It seemed natural that shortly after I met the woman
who was going to become my wife, I insisted that she
watch *Gunga Din* with me. It wasn't a test. It wasn't as

if I planned to give her a quiz at the end, like the football quiz in *Diner*. By chance, *Gunga Din* was showing on late-night TV, and I was sure she'd enjoy it. I'll admit that I harbored some fantasies about how we'd watch *Gunga Din* together in the years to come—laughing at Cary Grant's mugging and McLaglen's sputtering, sharing a shudder at the creepy leader of the murder cult.

My wife didn't seem terribly impressed by *Gunga Din*. She said that she didn't understand what distinguished it from *Four Feathers* and *The Lost Patrol* and other examples of a genre she referred to as "sand movies."

I thought about explaining how *Gunga Din* didn't have anything to do with movies like *The Lost Patrol*, and not just because it takes place in India, where there's no sand to speak of. But somehow I knew it wouldn't do any good. She would never see *Gunga Din* the way my father did. If we got married, it would be a marriage that did not provide me with a *Gunga Din* companion. My father had told me that *Gunga Din* was the greatest movie ever made, but he'd also told me that someday I'd probably meet a girl I'd be willing to give something up for.

My father, of course, was speaking before differences in movie tastes could be papered over with videocassettes. I now have my own tape of *Gunga Din*. The other day I was watching it when my wife, who was in another room, heard me laugh out loud.

"What are you doing?" she said.

"Watching *Gunga Din*," I said.

"Is it supposed to be funny?"

Just for a moment, I thought about telling her that *Gunga Din* was usually a lot better than it had been that night she saw it many years ago. I remember that print as looking jumpy and dark and—yes, I'll admit it—sandy. Also, the commercials came at awkward moments—for instance, right in the middle of the hilarious scene in which Cary Grant, hoping to stage a diversion so that Gunga Din can slip away to alert the regiment, emerges from where the two of them had been hiding in the murder-cult temple, strolls down the center aisle singing "All the roast beef from England and all the old English roast beef," and then announces to the horde of murder-cultists surrounding him that they're all under arrest. I thought about telling her that any movie can have an off night.

But I didn't think my wife had really built up sympathy over the years for the scene in which Douglas Fairbanks, Jr., whose term of enlistment is up, rejects the pleas of his fiancée in order to join Victor McLaglen in a two-man attempt to rescue Cary Grant from thousands of murder-cultists—leaving his fiancée to say, in a moment that blends exasperation with insight, "You'd rather be with him."

Also, my wife has always been understanding about my devotion to *Gunga Din*; she treats it the way she treats my lingering fondness for certain leftovers that my mother served me when I was a boy. You might say I have a *Gunga Din* easement. All in all, things have worked out.

"Yes, some of it is funny," I finally said. "But I don't actually think you'd like it."

March 28, 1994

I haven't told you yet about the pickpocket incident in Otavalo. I suppose I hesitated to say anything because, to be perfectly frank, I'm a little embarrassed by it.

In fact, for a while I considered not troubling you at all with the pickpocket incident in Otavalo. It happened, after all, in a relatively remote spot in Ecuador, and I figured that it was unlikely that anybody you knew was at the scene. But if there is one thing we've learned from the problems the White House has been having lately, it's this: anything that's embarrassing comes out sooner or later, even if it happened in the boonies.

A small city about an hour and a half north of Quito, Otavalo is set in a part of Ecuador where a visitor driving along the Pan American Highway can almost always see colorfully dressed Indians proceeding from town to town on foot, through valleys that have gorgeous green mountains in the background—although the visitor would do well to keep his eye on the road instead of looking at all of that, since a bus is almost certainly trying to pass him on a hill.

Otavalo is famous for its Saturday market. Actually, there are three markets. Very early on Saturday morning, there's an animal market just outside of town. I don't mean an animal market in the way you might describe one of these huge annual sales in a department store as an animal market, with a lot of people acting like animals. The people in this market are quite calm, and the animals they buy and sell are real animals.

Not much later, the main market begins in the streets and squares of the city: vendors selling everything from grain to hogs' heads to spare parts. In one area, spreading out from a place known as poncho plaza, the vendors sell the sort of items that tourists might be interested in carting home—ponchos, hammocks, sweaters, scarfs, purses.

In this market, a tourist may, after twenty minutes of hard bargaining, get an $11 sweater for only $10.20 and walk away feeling like someone who has just made a million or so in the commodities market—unless, of course, he discovers when it's time to consummate the deal that his wallet has been lifted. Otavalo, one of the most renowned weekly markets in Latin America, has a small collateral reputation for pickpockets.

I knew this. I had put my wallet in my side pocket— my defensive position. On the way to the market that Saturday, I reminded those in our party that they ought to be alert to hands in their pockets that were not their own. I reminded them that pickpockets in Ecuador, like pickpockets in most places, ordinarily work in a team, with a male jostler to stop and distract you while a female confederate lightens your load.

An hour or two later, as I was making my way through a narrow passage—someone had set up his roasted corn operation right in the middle of the street— a man bumped into me, blocking my way. "Excuse me," he said. "What time is it?" This was the first time since I'd arrived in Ecuador that anyone had bumped into me, the first time anyone on the street had addressed me in English, and the first time anyone had asked me what time it was.

Did alarm bells go off? Now we're getting to the embarrassing part. No alarm bells went off. The pickpocket warnings had vanished from my mind. I was, for all practical purposes, the yokel on his first visit to the state fair. I was going to tell the man what time it was. Here's the part that's slightly more embarrassing: I was going to tell him what time it was in Spanish.

It was, in fact, *diez menos cinco*. As I raised my wrist and read out the time to my new friend, a hand began groping at my side pocket. I felt it just in time to push it away. I can only imagine that it belonged to one of the clumsiest pickpockets in Latin America, someone known to her colleagues in the trade as Carmen the Klutz.

So there you have it. That's all there was to it. Oh, sure, I chastised myself later for being so dumb. Oh, sure, I imagined later how, if only I hadn't totally forgotten about pickpockets an hour after bringing up the subject, I might have, pretending to look at my watch, made a sudden gesture that caught Carmen by the wrist just as she reached into my pocket.

Still, I had my wallet. I had to be thankful for that. Also, I had an $11 sweater for which I had paid only about $10.20. There's nothing embarrassing about that.

April 4, 1994

For years we've been told that cultures differ in their notions of human beauty, so that someone considered an absolute knockout in the society of some remote island may be fat enough to be hooted off the streets of any American city. Now there is evidence from a study published in the British journal *Nature* that standards of beauty are, in fact, universal.

According to an account of the study in the *New York Times*, researchers showed pictures of faces to a number of men and women and asked the viewers to rank the faces by attractiveness. The viewers were in two groups—one Japanese and one Caucasian—and so were the faces being shown. If someone's notion of a beauty varies a lot according to whether he grew up in Kyoto or Manchester, the hypothesis went, the two groups of viewers should have had widely varying opinions about which faces were attractive. Showing the Japanese viewers a Caucasian face that the Caucasian viewers had found particularly attractive could presumably have resulted in shouts of "Cover that thing with a sack" or "That one got hit upside the head with an ugly stick" or whatever it is that Japanese shout in such circumstances.

That's not how it turned out. Whether the pictures were of Japanese faces or of Caucasian faces, the two groups of viewers agreed about which ones were the most attractive—high cheekbones and large eyes were the features everyone went for—and the researchers see that agreement as refutation of the "assumption that preferences for physical attractiveness are culturally dependent."

Is this further evidence that people are alike no matter where they come from and that we should therefore try to get along with each other and banish prejudice and give our extra change to UNICEF?

Maybe. But as it happens, some people who have spent years in, say, Springfield, Illinois, being considered not particularly attractive—people who have spent those years being described by arrangers of blind dates as having nice personalities—may have been holding out the hope that they would actually be considered quite attractive in the cultures of some place that sounds awfully far away, like Borneo or Zanzibar.

Somebody in Springfield who does not, in fact, have high cheekbones and large eyes—let's call him Norton—may have always had fantasies in which he is sitting in a sidewalk café in Zanzibar being eyed by a couple of attractive young women at the next table. Not realizing that he has made himself fluent in Swahili, they are discussing him openly. One of them is saying to the other, "Will you get a load of that gorgeous guy with the doughy face! Wow!"

"And those eyes," the other one says. "Did you ever see such slitty little piggy eyes? Those eyes are to die for."

"The man's a god."

If Norton read about the British study, he presumably began to face up to the possibility that traveling to Zanzibar might not improve his situation. If he listened to the conversation from the next table at a sidewalk café, he might, in fact, hear the phrase "nice personality" or even the phrase "hit upside the head with an ugly stick."

Studying the methodology of the study more carefully, Norton could comfort himself with its limitations.
In many ways, after all, Japan and Great Britain are no
longer that far apart culturally. The results show nothing
about societies that seem to vary more extremely from
the West in their idea of beauty, such as the African
tribes whose members seem to be wearing small salad
plates in their lower lips. On the other hand, if the alter-
native is to wear a small salad plate in the lower lip, many
people would prefer to be considered not particularly
attractive.

I can imagine Norton poring over the article, trying
to find some way that the study doesn't apply to him.
And then he realizes he has missed the most obvious fact:
the pictures that were shown to the viewers were pictures
of women's faces, not men's faces.

If there's a universal standard of female beauty, of
course, you might presume there is also one of male
beauty. On the other hand, the *Times* itself said that an
innate notion of female attractiveness might have
evolved through natural selection based on the association of certain facial characteristics with "youth and good
health, both of which are important to reproductive vitality."

If reproductive vitality is the issue, maybe youthful
facial characteristics are less important for men. Norton
knows that decrepit old codgers father babies all the time.
Norton puts aside the newspaper and stares into space.
He sees himself in his final Swahili lesson. He is flawlessly
translating the Swahili word for "hunk."

April 18, 1994

The recent physical assault on Barney in Worcester, Massachusetts, is more complicated than it at first appears. This is in itself discouraging. If even attacks on purple dinosaurs are more complicated than they at first appear, maybe everything is more complicated than it at first appears. Charlie Brown, who is normally in physical danger only while in the presence of Lucy, could express my response to that possibility with one word: "Sigh."

Barney is a character whose children's show on PBS has a tone characterized by a theme song that begins "I love you, you love me . . ." Apparently, many preschool kids believe Barney to be the first unequivocally good thing that has happened to them since some brute took away their pacifier.

Some grownups dislike Barney enough to have founded organizations like the We Hate Barney Secret Society. To these people, Barney is basically a large glob of schmaltz that has been painted purple.

Some parents, hounded by their children for the Barney dolls and Barney socks and Barney sheets sold by a Barney industry that is now estimated to make $100 million a year, view Barney as the most cuddly beast now permitted to engage in extortion in the United States.

PBS viewers who are aware that PBS managed to sign a contract to air Barney's show without getting so much as a nickel of the subsidiary rights may look upon Barney not as a glob of schmaltz but as a constant reminder that, but for the obtuseness of some high-paid public television executive, they could be spared from pledge weeks until approximately the year 2078.

Given the number of people who have grudges against Barney of one kind or another, then, it's no wonder that Barney attacks had been reported before, most recently at a store opening in Galveston, Texas. So the disruption of a drugstore's grand opening in Worcester, Massachusetts, by an attack on Barney—or, to be absolutely accurate, on a grown-up woman in a Barney costume; I might as well tell you right off the bat that purple dinosaurs do not actually exist—seemed to be a simple matter of Barney haters once again trying to pummel the object of their hatred.

Not exactly. It may have seemed that way if you read a two-inch wire-service bulletin on the incident. But the more thorough version I read in the *Boston Globe* reveals that this attack was not simply the equivalent of a heavy-metal fan tossing a pie at Barry Manilow.

In the first place, the young man who attacked Barney—a sophomore at a local college—apparently did so on a ten-dollar bet with one of his pals. Before pundits toss off some learned words about the level of hostility Barney engenders, they have to consider the possibility that the attacker didn't hate Barney at all.

He may just have needed the ten bucks. Or he may have been one of those college kids who will do just about anything on a dare—snatch the other team's mascot or sneak a slide of an exotic dancer into the slide carousel of the lecturer in History of Art 201: The Buildings of the Roman Era. For all we know, the attacker and his fraternity brothers may spend long Saturday afternoons on the porch singing "I love you, you love me . . ."

Beth Ryan, an official of the Barney Fan Club, interviewed by the *Globe* about this incident, said that it was particularly distressing because "Barney teaches people to love each other." But that turns out to be another assumption that begins to look less certain in a careful examination of the Worcester incident. According to the account in the *Globe*, the outrage provoked by the attack included "one youngster on the scene who volunteered to get a gun and execute the Barney beater."

Is it possible, then, that devotion to Barney is similar to devotion to some religious beliefs—something that sounds benign but can, at its extreme, turn you into a terrorist fanatic? Have the Congressional committees concerned with whether television inspires violence in young people checked out Barney?

While you're chewing on that one, consider this: Ms. Ryan, the Barney Fan Club official, was rather restrained in her sympathy for the woman attacked while wearing the Barney costume, because it was not a costume authorized and charged for by that supersweet Barney company that pulls in the $100 million. Commenting on the unauthorized costume, Ms. Ryan said, "What that woman did was grossly illegal."

Presumably, then, the defense the attacker might present in court is that he was attempting to thwart a crime in progress. I told you that this was complicated.

NERDS, UNVANISHED

A new book about vanishing Americana, *Going Going Gone*, is of some comfort to those of us who are old enough to remember the Second World War—if not as a war, at least as a paper drive.

The authors, Susan Jonas and Marilyn Nissenson, offer illustrated essays on about seventy former staples of American life, some of which I miss (two-newspaper towns, for instance, and the smell of burning leaves in autumn) and some of which I don't (men's garters, for instance, and the draft).

This provides a refuge from the seemingly endless palaver I hear about the information highway and the new technologies and the way everyone who owns a CD-Rom will soon be able to have his teeth filled without leaving his computer.

Some of the things discussed in the book are still seen here and there—drive-in movies, for instance, and penmanship and rotary phones. In fact, I happen to have a rotary phone myself, in the kitchen. I'm holding on to it, the way some people hold on to a twelve-foot plant stand their grandmother told them would surely be of great value someday. When the crunch comes, I'm going to tear that phone off the wall and take it right to a flea market. A flea market is already about the only place you'll find some of the items discussed in the book, in-

256] CALVIN TRILLIN

cluding the one that particularly interested me—the slide rule.

In the fifties, the slide rule was an essential piece of equipment to anyone studying math, but as a symbol it went way beyond that. As someone said to the authors of *Going Going Gone,* a slide rule was thought of as a "nerd-stick"—the weapon of choice for the unfortunate young men who had difficulty finding someone to accompany them to the prom or someone to choose them to play anything but right field.

It was to the nerd what a machete is to a cane cutter or an eye-loupe to a jeweler or a nightstick to a beat cop: he didn't wander forth without it. In those days, according to *Going Going Gone,* the largest manufacturer of slide rules was turning out twenty thousand of them a month. It now makes a hundred a year, mostly for collectors.

Does that mean that there are no more nerds? Did all of them get pounded into the ground like fenceposts by hulking football players? No, not at all. There are plenty of nerds left, some of them filthy rich.

Even the ones who aren't old enough to be filthy rich feel a lot better about themselves, despite the fact that they still may arrive at the prom solo. Why? Because symbolically what replaced the slide rule for nerds was not the device that literally supplanted it—the calculator, which carries no social implications whatsoever—but the computer.

Although the phrase "computer nerd" may still conjure up a vision of someone with thick glasses and an ungainly gait, it is a lot more respectful than anything a slide-rule carrier was called. Someone with a slide rule on his belt knew how to use a narrow-gauged instrument that nobody else cared much about. A computer nerd is assumed to have mastery over a device that has a huge and growing impact on the entire society—giving him almost enough clout to blot out the memory of those lonely afternoons in right field.

This turn of events made just about everybody happy, except maybe for slide-rule manufacturers and the sandlot superstars who found themselves seeking jobs from people they had once stuck in right field. A lot of the slide-rule carriers, after all, were smart and funny and better company than the guys picked first to play shortstop.

Lately, though, I've noticed some dark clouds. The day after I heard on the television news that a high school student in Long Island had been accused of using his computer bulletin board to lure much younger boys he wanted to molest, the *New York Times* carried a story about the indictment of an MIT student accused of using university computers to distribute a million dollars' worth of pirated software. If found guilty, the student could be sent to jail and fined $250,000.

There was a limit to the amount of trouble you could get into with a slide rule: it could probably have been used for slashing or poking, but slide-rule carriers weren't normally the slashing or poking types. In the fifties and sixties, MIT might have had to take some kidding about the prevalence of nerd-sticks on its campus, but at least nobody went to prison. Is this what's meant by the price of progress?

May 9, 1994

I am still contemplating the fact that Aureole, one of the most distinguished haute cuisine palaces on the East Side of Manhattan, was recently the site of a brawl.

From what a witness told the *New York Post*, two people from large parties bumped into each other and words were exchanged. Then, as they say at the ballpark, both benches emptied. The two sets of diners "were punching, overturning tables, throwing wine bottles—it was a bloody mess."

It used to be that your only risk in eating a fancy meal on the East Side of Manhattan was that you might find yourself dropping the money you had planned to use for your eldest's first semester at Princeton. Now we have to face the possibility that it might also be physically dangerous.

You say that the brawl at Aureole was an isolated incident? Maybe. It is interesting, though, that this happened during a spring that has also seen raucous picketing in front of yet another high-priced Manhattan restaurant, the Box Tree.

It is interesting also that during the same period strikers have been picketing the Harvard Club, where one of the issues, according to the *New York Times*, is management's proposal to end the ten-dollar "dirty job" bonus for "cleaning vomit, blood, excrement, etc."—an indication that the sort of contretemps that made the *Post* when it occurred at Aureole just once may be pretty much routine at the Harvard Club.

My friend Wayne, a close reader of the *Times*, told me that what bothered him about that list of what constitutes a dirty job at the Harvard Club was the "etc." The scenes that this word has conjured up in Wayne's mind do not bear dwelling upon.

You may be assuming right now that this discussion of danger is strictly hypothetical, since I have never struck you as the sort of person who patronized any of these eateries even before their perils included the possibility of being hit by a flying chair or of slipping on an unidentified substance.

You have misjudged me. I have been to all of them. I've had lunch a few times at the Harvard Club, and I thought the food was marginally less reminiscent of the Fort Dix mess hall than the food in some clubs. Still, when I read in the *Times* that one member who supported the strikers described himself as having spent $10,000 in meals at the club in 1993, it occurred to me that a man with a Harvard degree who has spent $10,000 on club food in a year only confirms the views of philistines who say that high-level education has no connection with common sense.

Some years ago, at a time when going to a fancy restaurant in New York still seemed a little more like having dinner and a little less like having your checking account cleaned out, my wife and I used to go to one fancy uptown joint or another once a year to celebrate her birthday—a custom that took us once to Aureole and once to the Box Tree.

I would go back to Aureole, although I'd prefer to

make the trip in the company of the sort of big butter-
and-egg man from the Midwest who gets insulted if you
reach for the check.

My experience at the Box Tree makes me wonder
why the place has never been picketed for pretentious-
ness. By far the most memorable part of the meal was
being presented the check in an old book whose pages
had been hollowed out to form a box for that purpose.

My wife said, "What a stupid idea"—or words to that
effect.

The man at the next table—meaning, since this is
the kind of place that bills itself as intimate, the man
practically sitting in our laps—said to my wife, "Are you
a librarian?"

The waiter huffed away, and returned to inform us
with some disdain, as he collected my credit card, that
delivering checks in books happened to be an authentic
custom of seventeenth-century somewhere.

"So was child labor," I said.

To be fair, I have to report that no fisticuffs ensued.
It was, after all, in the relatively nonviolent past of over-
priced restaurants.

I hate to think of what could happen these days. The
waiter might respond to my remark by saying "More coffee, sir?" and pouring some in my lap. The man at the
next table who assumed that anybody who is offended
by the mutilation of a book must be a librarian might
have thrown his crown roast in our direction, just as I,
finally pushed beyond the bounds of courtesy, overturned
his table. No one from the Harvard Club would appear
to clean up the mess.

June 6, 1994

The way I see it, some enterprising executive who would be willing to work for, say, ten or twenty million dollars a year, might be able to maneuver himself into a position to become CEO of the Walt Disney Company. Of course he'd have to play his cards right.

The thought that the CEO job at Disney might be available first occurred to me in 1988, during a protracted strike of Hollywood screenwriters. One of the issues in contention was the studios' insistence that because of the "new, colder realities facing the entertainment industry," the writers accept a rollback of the residual payments they were receiving.

In an article in *The New Yorker,* Joan Didion pointed out that the total received in residual payments by all nine thousand members of the Writers Guild was $58 million, and that the 1987 compensation of the Walt Disney Company's CEO, Michael Eisner, was estimated at $63 million.

The juxtaposition of those two figures cried out for a mathematical adjustment. You could almost hear the readers murmuring, "If the studios simply subtracted $58 million from Eisner's compensation to pay the residuals, the screenwriters would be happy, Eisner would still have $5 million a year to live on, and everyone could go back to work."

But Disney's board of directors couldn't have simply subtracted $58 million from Eisner's compensation. That would have indicated a lack of confidence in the CEO, and that, in turn, would have weakened the stock—including the stock of the directors.

So, for the good of the stockholders, it would have been better to replace Eisner than ask him to take a $58 million pay cut. That's why I thought some ambitious executive might, while having a round of golf with some members of the Disney board, mention that he would, if given Eisner's job at the same level of compensation, pay screenwriters' residuals for the entire industry out of his own salary, finance his own car and driver, and never put the National Secretaries Day flowers for his secretary on the expense account.

At the time, after all, there were, as there always are, five hundred executives considered capable of running a Fortune 500 company. As I remember the 1988 figures—*Business Week*'s annual issue on executive compensation has always been the one business publication I don't miss—people were running some of the top ten American corporations for as little as a few million dollars annually. Some CEOs may be less capable than others, of course, but $55 million a year less capable?

Disney directors apparently thought so. Eisner remained as the CEO who led the company into Euro Disney, which has now piled up debts of $4 billion despite the insistence of the Disney officials that it is attracting as many people as their projections indicated it would draw.

When I read about those projections being on target, I was reminded of a man in Nova Scotia I'll call Mr. Martin, who used to sell picnic tables for $15 until he discovered, after being urged by a friend to do some calculations, that the materials in each table were costing him $17. So this sort of thing can happen to anyone—although it should be said that nobody ever thought of paying Mr. Martin $63 million a year.

Now Disney wants to build another theme park, called Disney's America, near the Civil War battlefields of northern Virginia, and wants the state to pitch in $132 million for the necessary road improvements. Why should that worry a CEO who makes only half that much annually? Because $63 million is no longer Eisner's salary. The directors, apparently pleased as punch about Euro Disney, last year gave him a compensation package of $202 million. Part of this is incentive pay, of course, the theory being that if you paid an executive like Eisner only, say, $150 million, he might start not coming in on Fridays.

So Disney, in its public relations battle with opponents of Disney's America, is faced with another tempting juxtaposition of numbers. Virginians can see that if Eisner himself paid for the roads he'd still have a $70 million annual income. We already know he can live on that, because he managed to live on $63 million in 1988.

That is not the only embarrassment. A group of distinguished historians oppose Disney's America as a project that will "create synthetic history by destroying real history." The natural way to counterattack is to accuse the historians of being elitists who have lost touch with the common American. And who is the just-folks spokesman for that populist message? A man who pulls down $202 million a year.

Which is why I think this is the time for some wily executive to offer to do Eisner's job for, say, $10 million a year, enabling Disney to pay for the road improvements and have enough money left over to hire fifteen $4-million-a-year CEOs from other corporations.

After working for $10 million for a few years, the wily executive would be in position to go for the real money.

July 11, 1994
Today's mailbag is full of questions about Prince Charles, the Prince of Wales. Actually, that's not true. Today's mailbag is full of questions about the O. J. Simpson case. I'm ignoring those. I like to think of myself as a highbrow columnist who doesn't deal with that sort of thing, unless, of course, I can sneak it in under the guise of a column deploring all the sensationalist coverage.

Instead, I'm devoting this mailbag column to Prince Charles—which requires some imagination, because there is not one letter in the mailbag about Prince Charles. I'm discussing the prince's adultery, whether he is or is not what one letter writer refers to as a "dingbat," and whether he will succeed to the British throne or be passed over for Sting. Somebody around here has to practice serious journalism.

A Mr. G.R. from St. Louis, Missouri, writes, "Is this Charles guy a dingbat, or what?"

No, Mr. G.R., Charles is not a dingbat. It's often said that he is actually very nice, for a prince. Unlike a lot of royals, he doesn't mind having people who have never met him refer to him by his first name all the time, because he happens to be a first-name sort of guy.

Charles is so democratic, in fact, that he would actually prefer to be known as Chuck, the way William J. Clinton is known as Bill. Palace advisors thought that

Chuck would be inappropriate when his formal title was used, although Charles himself didn't see anything wrong with Prince Chuck, Prince of Wales, or even with King Chuck.

It's true that there are times when he, as the Shakespeareans used to say, "acts the dingbat"—that time at the truck factory in Sheffield, for instance. After the tour, the manager handed him a full glass; Charles, with a friendly "Well, here's mud in your eye," knocked it back; and then the manager said it was actually the new type of lubricating oil that had been responsible for a 1.5 percent increase in productivity.

Charles tells the story on himself, in a charmingly self-deprecating way ("Actually, the stuff wasn't half bad"). Some people think the fact that he tells such stories about himself shows just what a modest and unpretentious fellow he is, although others have warned of studies indicating that drinking lubricating oil can cause people to act like dingbats.

A reader from Parsons, Kansas, Ms. L.L., writes, "If everybody already knew that Prince Charles had been unfaithful to Princess Diana, why was it such a big deal that he said so on television? Wouldn't the British people rather have an honest person as king instead of some hypocrite?"

No, they wouldn't. One of the things people require in their leaders is a highly developed sense of euphemism. If Bill Clinton had gone on "60 Minutes" during the 1992 campaign and said, "Sure, I was playing around" instead of repeating that folderol about his marriage having gone through a troubled period, he would now be back in Little Rock wondering whether it was too late to start a career as a saxophonist who did federal-budget-policy patter between songs.

Remember what Senator Chuck Robb (formerly

Charles, but, by most accounts, not a prince) called similar episodes in his life? "Socializing under circumstances
not appropriate for a married man." That is leadership
talking.

Mr. R.W.A. of Akron, Ohio, writes, "Who but an
upper-class Englishman would sneak away from someone
who looks like Princess Di in order to play around with
someone who looks like Camilla Parker-Bowles? I mean,
talk about horsey! C'mon, gimme a break, willya."

I refuse to dignify that question with an answer. We
don't judge people on appearance. The question is in-
sulting not only to Ms. Parker-Bowles but to Princess Diana. Princess Di is not a sex object; she is more of a
clothes object. Ms. Parker-Bowles, described by the
prince as "a great friend of mine," is apparently a woman
of considerable accomplishment. We know from the in-
tercepted telephone conversation between her and the
prince, for instance, that she is quite good at talking dirty.
Mr. R.W.A.—who, by the way, is no great looker himself—ought to be ashamed to ask such a question.

In answer to Ms. J.F. of Canton, Ohio, it is not really
possible to know if Charles could succeed to the throne
if he divorced Diana and married a "fortyish midwest-
erner of Methodist background who loves walks in the
country, water-skiing, and reading by the fire." Also, I'm
not going to comment on whether the prince is "cutest
when he's blushing." Somebody around here has to practice serious journalism.

July 18, 1994

Picking through the newspaper the other day, trying my best to avoid being lectured once again on how O. J. Simpson symbolizes the way we treat heroes in our society or the pressure our society puts on African-American role models, I came across the name of Jeff Gillooly.

I had trouble getting the name in focus. Was Gillooly the guy sleeping on the couch when John Wayne Bobbitt had sudden cause to seek emergency room attention? Or was there a Dr. Gillooly testifying that the Menendez boys might well have pumped a lot of bullets into their mother as she watched television because they genuinely feared that any moment she might make them clean up their rooms?

Then I remembered: Tonya Harding's ex—from two cases ago. There was Tonya's ex in the newspaper again, like the ghost of tabloids past.

Of course. The attack on Nancy Kerrigan. It was a symbol of overcompetitiveness in sports, we were told by the analyzers, unless it was a reflection of class struggle in America. Whatever it symbolized, Gillooly has now been sentenced for his part in it to two years in prison.

If I may be forgiven for criticizing Jeff Gillooly at what must be a bad moment for him, I have to say that what stands out in my memory about the scheme he and his pals concocted to injure Nancy Kerrigan is how stupid it was. Of course it was vicious and cowardly and all that, but the dominant impression has to be dumbness.

At the time, in fact, what I wondered most about that caper was not whether it symbolized overcompetitiveness or the class struggle but why someone among the four or five people involved didn't say at some point in the planning process—if "planning process" is a term that can be applied to this operation—"Hey, guys, maybe this really isn't such a good idea."

This is the feeling I often get as I walk out of a Hollywood movie, irritated in equal parts that somebody was dumb enough to make such a movie and that I was dumb enough to sit through it. At some point in the development of this movie, couldn't somebody have understood that it was not such a good idea? I keep wondering why someone in some meeting didn't say, "I wonder if you fellows have noticed that the plot of this movie is absurd and the dialogue is childish."

Gillooly and his merry band apparently did not have such a person in their conferences. They went ahead and did what they had planned to do, and the fact that they had done it became obvious within, as I remember, about seventy-two hours. As the coverage of the incident began to become clearer in my mind, I found myself with another thought about Jeff Gillooly: what if he had been a little smarter?

What if Gillooly had planned the attack on Kerrigan so cleverly—as a start, employing someone who didn't brag about it to everyone standing around the Coke machine—that the police took six months to figure it out? What if the police had never figured it out?

Because for that first seventy-two hours, before the fingers began to point at the group of bozos gathered around Tonya Harding, what we were being told by the analyzers was that the attack on Nancy Kerrigan demonstrated the lunacy of sports fans. That's right. It was assumed to have been similar to the attack on Monica Seles. The heavy question being masticated in the columns was whether there is something about our society that turns fans into dangerous loony-birds.

Yes, the guy who stabbed Monica Seles was a German, but it was easy enough to find American examples of movie actresses who had been stalked and baseball players who had been harassed. I remember thinking at the time that we were in for enough of that sort of thing to make you feel guilty when you yelled "Go Knicks." Then the Gillooly Gang was fingered, and that was the end of learned essays on the psychology of someone who becomes fixated on an idol.

So does that mean that our society does not, in fact, turn fans into dangerous loony-birds? If O. J. Simpson did not, in fact, kill his wife and her friend, does that mean we can forget all of the stuff we've been told for the last month about heroes in our society and the pressure on African-American role models? If the next jury sends both Menendez boys up for first-degree murder, will we no longer be a society that makes victims out of perpetrators?

As Jeff Gillooly is sent off, I wonder. Meanwhile, it's hard to pick through the newspaper.

July 25, 1994
My wife and I have been having a little disagreement
about piping plovers. Don't worry. I think we can work
this out.

As you probably know, a piping plover is a roundish
little bird about the size of your fist. It is often found on
the beach—although not often enough these days, since
it is an endangered species. It is, according to ornitholo-
gists, an unusual subject for marital discord.

Marriage counselors always say to look for areas of
agreement. Fortunately, there are plenty of those. For
one thing, my wife and I both support the environmental
protection director of East Hampton, Long Island, who,
according to an item in the *New York Times* this spring,
has taken severe measures to protect nesting piping plovers. We both disagree with the fisherman who told the
Times reporter that maybe, in the grand progression of
nature, the piping plover was meant to become extinct
around now, in the way the dinosaur became extinct
some years ago.

To see how silly that idea is, you need only compare
a piping plover and a dinosaur. Go ahead: try to envision
a piping plover skeleton in some huge display hall in the
American Museum of Natural History and try to envision
a dinosaur on the beach in East Hampton. See what I
mean?

Also, my wife and I agree completely on the pronun-
ciation of "plover." We agree that it should be pronounced to rhyme with "rover," and that pronouncing it
to rhyme with "cover" is affected. If we meet someone
who pronounces plover to rhyme with cover, we both say,
in chorus, "Well, la-dee-dah."

I think it's accurate to say, in fact, that when it
comes to piping plovers our only area of disagreement is
whether or not we have ever seen any.

Here is my wife's case for her contention that we
have seen piping plovers. The beach we walk on, in the
Canadian Maritimes, has signs announcing that it is a
piping plover habitat. Also, some sections of the beach
are roped off as piping plover nesting areas. Also, we have
often seen roundish little birds that fit the description of
the piping plover printed on the signs. Otherwise, she has
no proof whatsoever.

I know what the counselor would say around now.
He would say that this disagreement reflects our personalities. He would say that my wife is a romantic person
who wants to believe in piping plovers and that I am a
cynic.

"I understand," he would say, "that when your wife
points out a common phenomenon like the Big Dipper
you say, 'It looks like just a bunch of stars up there to
me.' Also, I'm given to believe that you refer to all flowers
as marigolds."

Wrong. Well, O.K., that stuff about the marigolds is
right, although I prefer to think of it as a refusal to make
petty distinctions among flowers. But I don't say that
about the stars. What I think about the stars is that you
can make any design you want to out of them, so I say,
"And look over there. Is that Housemaid Dirndl or would
that be Plato's Lobster Tail?"

Also, I am not a cynic. I happen to believe deeply in

the existence of a bird called the mock plover—a roundish little bird, about the size of your fist, that is often
found on the beach.

"Your wife says that there is no such thing as a mock
plover," the marriage counselor would say.

"But until recently people thought there was no
such thing as the giant Muntjac deer," I'd say. "Now the
World Wildlife Fund has confirmed the existence of the
giant Muntjac deer in the Vu Quang nature reserve, in
Vietnam."

I happen to think that most of the birds we see on
our beach walks are mock plovers, although I am open to
the possibility that we might spot the occasional wood
thrush.

"Listen to that," my wife will say. "That is the char-
acteristic call of the piping plover."

"A wood thrush," I'll say. "That was the character-
istic call of a wood thrush."

"It was not a wood thrush."

"Did it have a sort of tweet-tweet-tweet sound?"

"Yes."

"Definitely a wood thrush."

"That's absurd," my wife will say. "The woods are a
mile from here."

"The wood thrush is known for the loudness of his
call," I'll say. "Many woodsmen carry a wood thrush with
them in a small cage on their belt, so that they can be
traced in the event they wander off too far in the woods.
Of course, it might have been a mock plover."

"There's no such thing as a mock plover."

"Well, I'll admit that its existence has yet to be confirmed," I'll say. "But we romantics continue to believe."
As you can see, I'm trying to work this out.

August 15, 1994

According to a quotation carried recently in the *New York Observer*, Jorge Luis Borges, the Latin American fantasist, was asked during a visit he once made to the NYU Institute for the Humanities what he thought of Sigmund Freud. "Never liked him," Borges said. "Too *schmutzig*."

I was among the readers who found that response surprising. When I was growing up in Kansas City, the few references to Freud that drifted my way gave me the impression that what he wrote was *schmutzig*, or dirty (in that period of my life, I'm not sure that anything would have struck me as *too* dirty), and this is the first evidence I've come across that in those days I was thinking along the same lines as Jorge Luis Borges on any subject at all. Also, the fact that Borges would use a homey Yiddish word like *schmutzig* required me to make some adjustments on the image of him that I had been carrying in my mind. It's as if I had been informed that distinguished literary personages who called on Henry James in his London drawing room were customarily greeted with a cheery "Hey, goombah!"

I should say that, now that I'm grown up, I no longer associate Freud's writings with smut. These days, my views on Freudianism are virtually identical to my views on Presbyterianism: some people believe in it, I was brought up not to be disrespectful of other people's beliefs, and for all anybody knows, it could turn out to be right on the money.

I was therefore not someone who took particular satisfaction in the discovery, made some years ago, that Freud had fudged some data in order to come up with his seduction theory, which is central to Freudian thought. I'll admit that I was interested in the controversy provoked by that discovery, in the way I'd be interested in what Presbyterians would have to say if it were discovered that their belief in predestination was the product of an unfortunate misunderstanding at the printer's in 1536.

Either case would bring up what I think of as the Davis Conundrum—how to deal with information that may call into question a tenet that is central to a system of belief. The Davis Conundrum takes its name from a wine-tasting test that I'm told is sometimes given at the renowned department of oenology at the University of California at Davis. It turns out that under blind-test circumstances the tasters, some of them professional wine connoisseurs, are often unable to tell red wine from white. That triggers the Davis Conundrum: does the failure to distinguish red from white undercut all the learned talk you hear about body and vintage and integrity and which side of the hill the grapes came from?

I assume that there have already been any number of seminars on the question of whether the seduction theory's being based on incorrect data invalidates the Freudian theories that followed. The recent publication of the first volume of *The Correspondence of Sigmund Freud and Sándor Ferenczi* is likely to provoke even more seminars. In these letters to a trusted disciple, Freud, not surprisingly, has some critical words to say about his rival, Carl Jung. You might expect him to write, "Jung, of course, is transferring to me his suppressed infantile homoerotic attraction for his Uncle Heinrich," or words to that effect. Not at all. According to what I read in the *New York Times Book Review*, here is what Freud wrote to Ferenczi about Jung: "Jung is *meshuga*."

Meshuga, of course, means crazy in Yiddish, and I must say that I was delighted to hear that Sigmund Freud as well as Jorge Luis Borges employed that dazzlingly expressive language, which many German-speaking Jewish bourgeois have scorned. This raises the possibility that Freud's grandson—the renowned artist Lucian Freud, whose paintings of not altogether beautiful people were such a hit not long ago at the Metropolitan Museum of Art—may have as a child called the great doctor *zayde*. For some reason, contemplating that possibility makes me feel better about both of them.

On the other hand, could this actually be Sigmund Freud's diagnosis of Carl Jung—"Jung is *meshuga*"? When the founder of psychoanalysis offered his opinions in a private letter rather than in a paper designed to be read by the profession at large, was this the way he talked? If that's the case, his frank, personal opinion of any one of his most celebrated analysands might have been (translated from his vernacular to ours), "The man's bonkers—off his squash, nutty as a fruitcake, a cuckoo bird." If so, what's all this talk about sublimation and Oedipus complexes and penis envy? As Jorge Luis Borges might have put it, why did we need all that *schmutz*?

HAT TRICK

Did I go to London to stretch my Kansas City Blues baseball cap on an antique hat stretcher? Well, yes, sort of.
That's not what I said to the immigration officer, of
course. When he asked me the purpose of my visit to the
United Kingdom, I said tourism. I always say "tourism"
to immigration officers, no matter what I'm up to. It's
one of my policies.

On the plane I had tried to imagine what would happen if a customs inspector who was searching my luggage
ran across my hat and said, "What's this, then?"

"That, sir, is an authentic replica of a Kansas City
Blues baseball cap, circa 1949," I'd say, wondering
whether I might be accused of trying to avoid some value-
added tax if I admitted that it was being brought in for
stretching purposes.

"Is that the year the Blues won the American Association pennant, leaving the Louisville Colonels and
the Minneapolis Millers in their dust?" I'd imagined him
saying.

"No, that was 1947," I'd say, "but how does a British
customs inspector happen to know about triple-A baseball in the Midwest in the 1940s?"

"I'm actually doing this part-time while I work on
my doctorate in American Studies at Reading University.
My dissertation is on Hank Bauer."

"Rugged ex-marine Hank Bauer?" I'd say, automatically prefixing the name in the manner made obligatory by the sports page of the *Kansas City Star*. "He was part of the 1947 outfield, along with Cliff Mapes and . . . and . . ."

"Eddie Stewart," the customs inspector would say. Then he'd hold up my baseball hat to admire it. "How does it look on?" he'd say.

"We'll see."

In fact, nobody searched my luggage. The hat did not come up when the immigration officer at Heathrow and I had our little chat. He seemed satisfied to hear that I had come for tourism. I was, of course, not wearing my hat at the time. It needed stretching before I could wear it comfortably; that was the whole point. Our friend Mary, who lives in London, happens to have an antique hat stretcher, in working order, and I intended to make use of it.

I wasn't lying to the immigration officer. I did some of the things tourists do. I ate fish and chips, for instance—a very English custom, although the fish-and-chips place I went to, a renowned spot called Nautilus, fries its fish in matzoh meal.

I wasn't wearing my baseball cap at Nautilus. If I had been, I suspect the proprietor would have admired it. He might have asked me if I thought his restaurant would be making a shrewd promotional move to put out a baseball hat of its own—maybe one that included a motto like "Where the Haddock Meets Its Matzoh."

Also, I went to the Barbican Centre to see the Royal Shakespeare Company do *The Tempest*. The Barbican Centre is what Americans would call a multi-use facility—a vast and baffling place where a lot of people who think they're in line to pick up their tickets are actually heading toward the snack bar or the parking garage.

Nobody has any trouble understanding the Shake-
spearean language in Royal Shakespeare Company productions these days: compared to the signs around the
Barbican, it's as clear and simple as the conversation with
the waitress at Nautilus. As if things there weren't con-
fusing enough already, a note in our program announced,
"The re-numbering of the floors will take place in the
summer." It presented a list that included the information that the fifth floor would be the ground floor and
the third floor would be the Stalls Floor or -1.

I regretted not having my baseball hat with me. Before the play and during the intermission, a lot of Americans were wandering around looking lost—I don't think
they had any idea whether the renumbering of the floors
had already taken place or not—and they probably would
have been comforted by a little triple-A baseball nostalgia.
But my hat hadn't been stretched yet.

I had no intention of stretching it all the way to the
next size. A hat the next size might fall off if I went after
a long fly ball, I explained to Mary when I finally made
it over to her hat stretcher.

"Are you going after a lot of long fly balls these
days?" Mary asked.

"You can never tell," I said.

She put the hat on the hat stretcher—a polished
wooden skull consisting of two hemispheres that could
be moved apart—and then we turned the lever just
enough to make the stretcher a touch larger. Then we all
had dinner. Then I tried on my hat. It was perfect. From
a certain angle, I thought I looked just a little bit like
rugged ex-marine Hank Bauer.

SIGN WRITING

November 21, 1994
For people who make their living as writers, the routine messages of everyday life have to be put together with some care. You don't want to leave rough drafts lying around. I've known novelists for whom the prospect of composing a note asking that a son or daughter be excused from gym that day can bring on a serious case of writer's block.

I was reminded of that recently when our car had to be left on city streets for a few days, and I, attempting to benefit from the experience of a couple of trips in the past to AAAA Aardvark Auto-Glass Repair, took on the task of composing a sign to inform potential pillagers that it contained nothing of value. Hours later, my wife happened to ask me to do some little chore around the house and I heard myself saying, "I can't right now. I'm on the fourth draft of this car sign."

There was no reason for her to be surprised. She has seen me stuck badly on an RSVP. In fact, routine social communication can be particularly knotty for writers, since they habitually try to express themselves in ways that are not overused. This is why a biographer who seems capable of producing a 1,200-page volume in fairly short order can often be inexcusably late with, say, a simple thank-you note.

Reading over what he's put on paper, he'll say to

himself, "I can't believe that I wrote anything as lame as 'Thanks for a wonderful weekend.' " Then he'll put aside the entire project until a more original phrase comes to him. A few weeks later, while the draft is still marinating on the writer's desk, the weekend's hostess feels confirmed in her impression—an impression that began to surface with the wine-spilling incident on Saturday night—that the biographer is a boor or a yahoo.

What my fourth draft of the car sign said was "No Radio." I thought that was spare and to the point, without extraneous language. I came to it from "No Radio or Any Other Valuables," which I decided, after some reflection, protested too much.

"What do you think?" I asked my wife, handing her the sign.

"It's O.K.," my wife said. "I saw some ready-made signs for car windows at the hardware store, and that's what one of them said, so I guess it's what people think is effective."

"You saw the same sign, worded in just that way?"

"I'm not saying you plagiarized it from the hardware store."

"Actually, I haven't been in there in some time," I said.

"It's really O.K.," my wife said. " 'No Radio' is fine."

It's fine if you're satisfied to be writing at the same level as some gorilla at the sign factory. Thinking I needed some fresh ideas, I phoned my older daughter, who lives just around the corner. "What would be a good sign to put in the car to discourage crackheads from smashing the window so they can get at six cents in change on the floor and the spare fan belt and an old pair of pliers?" I asked.

My daughter, a survivor of one of those earnest and

progressive nursery schools in Greenwich Village, said, "How about 'Use Words Not Hands'?"

This was a reference to what the teachers at her nursery school were constantly saying as the little monsters attacked one another with any weapon at hand. At one point we all began to wonder exactly what the words for sneaking up behind another kid and pulling her hair might be.

It wouldn't surprise me at all if that hair-puller had turned to a life of petty crime. As much as I enjoyed contemplating the look on his face when he spotted his nursery-school slogan on a car he was about to break into, I decided that the impact of "Use Words Not Hands" rested on the sort of allusion that an editor would criticize as "too inside."

The next draft was a complete departure—more of a new approach, really, than another draft. It said, "There Is Nothing of Value Here." Upon reflection, I decided that it sounded too philosophical. I could picture a car thief who came upon it turning to his partner in crime and saying, "Talk about pretentious!"

So now I'm sort of stuck. Meanwhile, the car's on the street. It is not completely without protection. An old shirt cardboard taped onto the backseat window bears the words "Sign in Preparation."

October 10, 1994

The kid and I were going to be together for a while—I was giving him a ride from his grandmother's back home—so I knew we'd get on the subject of video games sooner or later. It surprised me, though, that we were hardly out of the driveway before he said, "My favorite video game is Killer Krunchup, where you can stab the guy and tear his arm off at the same time."

"Listen," I said, "I don't mean to criticize, but aren't there supposed to be some warm-up questions before we start talking about video games?"

The kid shrugged.

"As I remember the way these conversations go," I went on, "I'm supposed to ask you some questions about how school's going this year, and how you like your teacher—that sort of thing. And you're supposed to answer O.K. to everything. Just O.K. Then, after a few long, awkward silences, we get to video games."

"School's O.K., the teacher's O.K.," the kid said.

"Well then," I said, "what's your favorite video game?"

"Killer Krunchup," the kid said. "Before you stab the guy and tear his arm off at the same time, you can pop each of his fingers out of their sockets and feed them to a rottweiler, but you have to be careful because once the rottweiler has those fingers he always jumps at the hero's throat. It's cool."

"Killer Krunchup is not my favorite video game," I said. "Although I'll admit that the finger-feeding is a good touch. It's as if the fingers are appetizers for the rottweiler and the jugular vein is the main course."

"You play video games?" the kid asked, sounding as if he found that exceedingly difficult to believe.

"Do I look to you like a person who does not play video games?" I said.

"Actually, yes," the kid said. "You look like your hand–eye coordination isn't what it used to be."

"Looks are deceiving," I said. "As it happens, I'm one of the best in our neighborhood at a video game called Sofa Warrior. Did you ever play that?"

"I never heard of Sofa Warrior," the kid says. "What happens in it? Do people kill each other with sofas or does the warrior use the sofa as a shield while he shoots poisoned darts into the villains or does he jump off the sofa the way you jump off a trampoline and then kill the bad guys and tear their throats out?"

"No, actually, that's not the way it works," I said. "The way it works is that the hero starts out lying on the sofa, with a pillow over his head. He's taking a nap. And a lot of people try to get him off the sofa. His wife wants him to mow the lawn and one of his kids wants him to play catch in the back yard and another kid wants to talk to him about buying a sweater. They keep trying to pull the pillow off his head, and he has to grab it back. It happens to take a lot of hand–eye coordination."

"But who gets killed?" the kid asked.

"Well, nobody gets killed, but harsh words are spoken," I said.

"It sounds kind of boring," the kid said. "Is that the only video game you play?"

"Well, no, now that you mention it," I said. "I play Refrigerator Raider."

"Is that about a raider who's like a commando raider, and he's as big as a refrigerator?" the kid asked.

"Close," I said. "The raider is not as big as a refrigerator but he's, well, maybe a little chunky. He's trying to open the refrigerator to get at some leftover macaroni-and-cheese—or, in some versions of the game, a turkey leg and some cold potatoes—and various people are trying to close the refrigerator door before he can get out the food."

"Is there a rottweiler?" the kid said.

"Nobody eats leftover rottweiler," I said. "Not even Refrigerator Raider."

"Not leftover," the kid said. "I was thinking maybe the rottweiler would be guarding the refrigerator, and if the raider didn't move fast enough the rottweiler would tear his throat out."

"You don't think it's exciting enough that the raider has to be on the lookout for his wife, who sometimes hides in the breakfast nook and leaps out to slam the refrigerator door and tell the raider that not only can't he have any macaroni-and-cheese, which he really loves, but that he has to mow the lawn?"

The kid just sighed, and shook his head.

"So how's school going this year?" I asked.

May 1, 1995

The people in my neighborhood—Greenwich Village, in lower Manhattan—have a new problem. Our subway stop is being made beautiful, and we haven't figured out how to complain about it.

The phrases that trip most easily off the tongues of New Yorkers are expressions of complaint. If a linguistic anthropologist camped out in Manhattan for a while, I suspect he'd discover that New Yorkers have fifty or sixty different phrases for expressing irritation and maybe two for expressing enthusiastic approval ("Not that bad" and "It could be worse").

The average subway rider would associate expressions of enthusiasm with people he'd describe as being from "Indiana or Idaho or one of them." (As I have pointed out before, true New Yorkers do not distinguish among states that begin with the letter "I.") For generations—long before the great cities of this country became associated in the public mind with their problems rather than their wonders—New Yorkers have believed in the old saying that they learn at their mother's knee: "If you can't say something nice, you're never in danger of being taken for an out-of-towner."

This is not the first time the Metropolitan Transportation Authority has presented us with an awkward situation: in recent years all of the old subway trains in

New York have been replaced with shiny new silver trains that are absolutely free of graffiti. They are also air-conditioned.

If you live outside New York—or if you are one of those thick-headed New Yorkers who prefer traffic jams to subway travel—you are probably thinking that the preceding paragraph was one of my little jokes. It wasn't. The New York subways really do have flashy new cars, but New Yorkers rarely mention that fact. It's a difficult thing to complain about.

Not impossible. I've heard a lot of people complain that the absolutely frigid air-conditioning in the subway cars makes the stations, which are still not air-conditioned, seem even hotter than they are. I've heard people say that they miss the graffiti—which is apparently cleaned off at the end of every run, so that there isn't much reason to put it on in the first place—and resent the censoring of this urban folk art by the philistines who run the MTA.

It is also possible to complain about how the decision to acquire new cars was made—or, to put that thought in the local vernacular, how the MTA unilaterally and high-handedly, without consulting the people who actually use the subways every day, decided to force comfortable and attractive new subway cars on the public.

Improvements in the transportation system rarely meet with the approval of New Yorkers. Some years ago, the then-mayor, Edward Koch, came back from China smitten with the idea of bicycle transportation. He had protective strips of concrete installed to create a bicycle lane up Sixth Avenue. Eventually they were removed. People had complained.

I mentioned at the time that you might have expected the taxi drivers to hate the mayor's innovation, since it had cost them basically one lane of traffic ("He likes China so much, he shoulda stood in China"). But who complained most bitterly about the bike lanes? The bicyclers.

The true New York bicyclers—particularly the messengers—complained that the bike lane was full of pedestrians and garment-center pushcarts and bike riders who were described as "schlepping around on Raleigh three-speeds."

"Schlepping" is Yiddish, a language that all true New Yorkers—including Irish cops and Dominican grocers and Pakistani newsdealers—speak a little of, partly because its rhythms are famously conducive to complaint. One Yiddish word that all New Yorkers are familiar with is "kvetch," which actually means "to complain." You often hear them say to each other, "Quit kvetching"—to no apparent effect.

So you can see the sort of problem my neighbors and I faced as workmen in our station replaced worn tiles and restored lovely old mosaics. At first we made do with complaining about the pace of the work ("Are they ever going to finish this place?"). A couple of people tried to argue that the stunning new floor would be slipperier than the grungy old floor. By last week, though, it was obvious that our station was going to be gorgeous.

The other day, while a neighbor and I waited for an uptown local, I decided that I had to express my approval of the renovations, even at the risk of being taken for somebody from Iowa or Illinois (I'm from Missouri). "Not that bad," I said, gesturing toward the shiny tiles and the stunning new floor.

My neighbor looked around. "It could be worse," he admitted. "But where in the hell is the train?"

People can't seem to get it through their heads that a newspaper columnist is infallible. They keep sending in corrections. Without listing every single correction I've received concerning the foregoing columns—that sort of thing just encourages phrases like "riddled with errors"—I'll deal with a couple of representative examples. It should surprise no one that they are representative partly in that they both deal with animals.

I include oysters in the category of animals, although I've never heard the charge of cruelty to oysters hurled at anyone—not even at someone who eats them alive by the dozen. Joyce Taylor, a seafood education specialist with the University of North Carolina Sea Grant College Program, wrote that I was too quick to take comfort from a Louisiana State University study indicating that the sort of hot sauce that people in Louisiana eat on raw oysters is effective in killing a wicked bacterium called *Vibrio vulnificus*. The LSU results showed the efficacy of Louisiana hot sauce against *Vibrio vulnificus* only in laboratory cultures, Ms. Taylor reminded me.

I immediately called my Louisiana oyster-eating friend, Armand, a man whose reverence for oysters that are found in his state's waters rivals the feeling that some Kentuckians have about Kentucky whiskey. I felt it was my duty to tell him that a seafood education specialist in

North Carolina was recommending that raw oysters be avoided until there's proof that hot sauce works equally well in human stomachs.

"I don't blame someone in North Carolina for avoiding oysters," Armand said. "I'd avoid them too if I had to live there. North Carolina oysters taste like marshmallows that have been fished out of the pool at the YMCA."

Armand's response was, of course, completely wrongheaded—the UNC recommendation has nothing to do with the quality or origin of oysters—and extremely rude. I apologize to Ms. Taylor on his behalf. All I can say in his defense is that he's been acting odd lately. Some of us are thinking of asking LSU to undertake a study on whether Louisiana hot sauce increases irascibility as it kills bacteria.

The other correction was really more of an addendum. It was from James Edmunds, a friend of mine from New Iberia, Louisiana, whose friendly demeanor would indicate either that Louisiana hot sauce does not, in fact, cause irascibility or that James has been staying off the stuff. James writes a column himself, and you might say his addendum was in return for my advice on a piece he published in the *Times of Acadiana*. In that piece, he revealed that he has been thinking of launching a 900 number to answer questions about whether various prominent Americans are still alive. He calls it the National Dead Line. Once the National Dead Line is established, there will be an easy way to satisfy your curiosity about, say, the leading man in an old movie you've been watching on television. When the movie is over, you simply pick up the telephone and dial 1-900-WHODEAD.

According to the plan James had mapped out, someone who calls the National Dead Line will get not a simple yes or no but an answer that is calibrated to degree of certainty. This could range from "Definitely dead—November 9, 1989, of heart failure, at eighty-four, in Camden, New Jersey," to "He was just on 'Good Morning America' this morning." I told James that "Possibly dead" might sound better than "If he's not dead, he sure is quiet." I also cautioned him against including as one possible calibration "Extremely dead," which I thought was in questionable taste.

James called to comment on a column I had written about the untimely demise of the chicken—Willy by name—that used to play tic-tac-toe so successfully against human beings in Chinatown. I had mentioned that a reference in the *New York Times* to the company that had trained Willy—Animal Behavior Enterprises, of Hot Springs, Arkansas—seemed to lend credence to the claims made for years by the writer Roy Blount, Jr., that he had met the chicken's trainers in Arkansas and that they were former graduate students of B. F. Skinner, the noted Harvard behaviorist.

What James had to add to the mix was this: No more than half a dozen years before, while passing through that very same Hot Springs, a town that has had a reputation for offering visitors a range of racy entertainment, he had occasion to stop at a place called the I.Q. Zoo. James is keen on animals. There he saw a chicken playing basketball and rabbits putting on a wild-west show. He has always remembered the visit warmly. When other people recalling their own visits to Hot Springs might mention coming across a game of chance or something even naughtier, James presumably says, "You sure missed a sight when those little bunnies unholstered their six-guns."

With James's help, I got in touch with Mark Duncan, the proprietor of a Hot Springs enterprise called Educated Animals, who confirmed Blount's story about how tic-tac-toe–playing chickens had originated. Some years

ago, Duncan told me, two of Skinner's former graduate
students founded Animal Behavior Enterprises, which
trained animals for government work—dolphins sniffing
out enemy subs and that sort of thing—as well as for
entertaining the sort of people who have always wondered just how fast on the draw a rabbit could be.

The I.Q. Zoo had been part of Animal Behavior Enterprises, Duncan told me. Both are out of business now,
he said, but people in the trade all over the country can
trace their training back to those operations. He himself
learned the ropes from someone who had worked for
someone who started out at A.B.E. "You might say I'm
a third-generation animal trainer," he said. "Fourth if you
count Skinner."

At Educated Animals, Duncan told me, he offers,
among other attractions, a parrot that rides a scooter, a
macaw that plays dead, a raccoon that shoots baskets in
answer to mathematical problems (you ask what two and
two equals, he shoots four baskets), a rabbit that shoots
off a cannon, a Vietnamese pig that drives a Cadillac, a
rooster that walks a tightrope, and a chicken that dances
while a rabbit plays the piano and a duck plays the guitar.

A raccoon that shoots baskets in answer to mathematical problems? That one stopped me. I had to measure that against the advice by the old-timer in our town
that a combination lock is effective against raccoons because "they're cunning but they've got no head for figures." Here was strong evidence from someone trained
by someone who was trained by someone who was
trained by B. F. Skinner that raccoons may have a head
for figures after all. I am rethinking my entire raccoon
defense perimeter. I recommend that readers do likewise.